A
Mid-Wales Family

by

Glennys Orlando Jones

with period photographs

and line drawings by Jane Keay

Published by Great Oak Bookshop, Llanidloes, Powys

Printed by St. Idloes Press, Llanidloes, Powys

November 1994

ISBN 0 9524653 0 2

For my nieces Gwen and Tessie

who grew up in Africa.

PREFACE
AND ACKNOWLEDGEMENTS

This book was intended as a simple record of my parents' reminiscences. I began setting down what I could remember for the sake of my niece who grew up in Africa. Gradually the account has been enlarged and enriched through the generosity of many people. I hope that others may be interested in the picture it presents of a vanished way of life as seen by an ordinary Mid-Wales family. I am deeply grateful to Mrs. Curigwen Cruikshank and Mr. John Cruikshank for permission to quote extensively from Professor E.Arthur Lewis' book, **Rhai Atgofion Yr Hen Ysgol, Pantmawr.** Lt. Com. Cenarth Davies and Mr. Howell Davies have kindly allowed me to use the early section of their mother's Memoirs, which appears as Part Three of this book, and have also supplied family photographs. The late Mr. Noel Jerman not only allowed me to quote from his book, **Kerry - the Church and the Village,** and from his Presidential Address to the Cambrian Archaeological Association - he regaled me with tea and stories of Kerry in his schooldays. Others to whom I am similarly indebted for hospitality, personal recollections and further information include:
Miss Monica Price, Red House, Llandinam; Miss Lucy Waite, Yew Tree Cottage, Llandinam; Mrs. M.J. Morgan, Idloes Terrace, Llanidloes, who related her memories of Pantmawr School, and permitted me to use her copy (possibly the last) of Professor Lewis' book; Mr. Bill Jones, Rhosgoch, Pantmawr, who allowed me to tape-record him as he spoke of the life of the district, past and present; the late Mr. Idwal Turner, Hillfield, Llanidloes and Mr. Alan Mills, Llanerch, Llangurig, who helped to clarify events in Llangurig, and Professor I.G. Jones, Laura Place, Aberystwyth who gave me most helpful information and advice.

I owe a special debt to the Governors of three of the schools in which my mother taught, and to the Headmasters who made time to enable me to use the Log Books and Registers : Mr. Lewis, B.Sc., of Castle Caereinion, Mr. Nigel Catley of Kerry and Mr. D.M.Williams of Llandinam - Thank You! Thanks likewise to Mr. Richard Morgan, B.A., Powys County Archivist who made the records of Dolforwyn, Llangurig and Pantmawr Schools available. The Librarians and Staff of the National Library of Wales, and of Newtown, Bargoed and Merthyr Tydfil made my researches a pleasure.

I have been most fortunate in having two friends with a deep interest in local history, who have generously shared with me the results of their own research, copies of documents, and many striking and relevant photographs. They are Mr. Brian Rollings, The Old Vicarage, Llangurig, and Mr. E. Ronald Morris, B.A., Maen Hinon, Y Gilfach Uchaf, Gorn Road, Llanidloes, who is well-known as a historian of the Mid-Wales area. Mr. Morris also translated Prof. Arthur Lewis' book, and gave me detailed advice.

For her constant interest and support, and for her patience on my various expeditions I wish to thank my friend, Mrs. Gwyneth Jenkins, 9, Maes yr Ysgol, Llanidloes.

The visual impact of this book has been enhanced by photographs from many sources. To those who have allowed me to use pictures from their personal collections, and to the Library Staffs for permission to reproduce from their Archives I express my gratitude: The National Library of Wales, Aberystwyth; St. Fagan's Folk Museum; Bargoed Library; Miss Lucy Waite; Miss Monica Price; Mrs. Jean Nash; Mrs. Norah Dailey; Mrs. Rees, Nantyrhendy; Mr. Alan Mills; Mr. Brian Rollings; Mr. Farmer, Black Lion Hotel, Llangurig; Mr. Ronald Morris; Mr. John Nesbitt, Tylwch, Mrs. J. Ellis.

Jane Keay's illustrations, so entirely in sympathy with the story, add an extra pleasure. To Jane and her husband Roger I am grateful for their belief that our joint enterprise was worthwhile.

Finally I am especially indebted to Dr. Andy Scrase of the Great Oak Bookshop who generously decided to take the risk of publishing the book, and to Mr. Robert Edwards and the staff of St. Idloes Press for their patience and help in producing it.

CONTENTS

NOTES

BIBLIOGRAPHY

APPENDIX

Llangurig from Foel hill about 1890. In foreground the old tollgate house.
Photo shows "new" Nonconformist cemetery open in 1886, the old M.C. Chapel (Penybont) which gave way to present chapel in 1904-5.

LLANGURIG CHURCH.

E. SALTER, DEL.

D. MARPLES, LITH., L'POOL.

Llangurig Church. Lithograph based on a painting by E. Salter 1975 prior to 1877-1880 restoration of the Church. *By permission of the National Library of Wales.*

Llanwrin Church c. 1890

Chapter 1.
Home, School and Sunday School

My father started school (in 1896) at 3½ years of age. This was the age at which all the children in the family, except the eldest daughter, Mary, first went to school - and I can well understand my grandmother's relief at getting one more little one from under her feet for a few hours. They lived next door to the school, so Grandma simply took him by the hand, opened the door of the Infants' room, thrust him in, closed the door and went home.

The teacher, Mrs. Jane Davies, a kindly young woman, came forward to receive him. But the little lad, in a strange and frightening environment, saw this as a threat.

She took his hands, so he lashed out with his feet. He was wearing a new pair of boots, hob-nailed, naturally, and he caught her on the shin. She fell to the floor, and before my father could escape he was seized by the other children, and the Headmaster was fetched. Mr. Rowbotham arrived with his stick, and administered a few sharp strokes to bring this young rebel under control.

So there my father remained until Playtime came. As soon as they were released into the yard he marched out through the gate, and up the road. A few minutes later he was seen trudging back through the gate, dragging behind him a huge 'traws' - a branch - from a hedge which was being laid up the road.

The older boys, including two of his brothers, surrounded him, demanding what he was going to do with it.

"I'm going to thrash the Headmaster," he replied.

Everyone laughed, including the teachers who were watching through the window.

Grandma could easily have seen this part of the incident from her back-kitchen window. They lived in two adjoining houses, Numbers 1 and 2, Wesley Row. Mrs. Williams lived in Number 3, and next to that was the Wesleyan Chapel. Beyond the Chapel was a little cottage where Marged Morgan lived, and in front of that was the well, which they shared, until Grandpa saw Marged washing articles which shall be nameless at the well. He then had a pump installed behind their home, so they didn't use the well any more.

Just beyond Marged's cottage was Grandpa's workshop, a timber structure which he had bought from someone in Rhayader when he decided to set up as a tailor in Llangurig. The front room of the first house was used as a shop, where Grandma sold socks, stockings, Holdfast boots and shoes, laces, needles and thread etc., the boots hanging from the edges of the shelves and from the ceiling.

The other front room was used as the parlour or living room, and it is this room that I remember.

As you opened the front door, on your left was the harmonium. Next to that along the wall stood the kitchen-piece, of medium oak, a lovely golden brown colour, filled with blue and white china. In the corner hung a corner cupboard, with lustre jugs and china ornaments.

Opposite the front door was the door to the back-kitchen, and next to that the beautiful Grandfather clock, made in St. Harmon's with its polished dark oak case and shining brass face. A cupboard was fitted into the recess between the clock and the fire-place, and this held books and music.

The fire-place consisted of a small iron range - a high-standing grate with bars in front, and oven and boiler on either side. This was always black-leaded, and the brass handles shone. The bars at the front of the grate were ideal for making toast, and from the hooks above the fire hung the kettle. A mantel-piece surmounted the range, and on this were brass candle-sticks and other ornaments.

Under the window to the right of the front door stood a scroll-ended horse-hair sofa, and in front of the fire were two arm-chairs of the Windsor style. Behind these, in front of the kitchen-piece, was the table and straight-backed chairs.

The children didn't usually have their meals in this room when they were small, for it seems to have been reserved for Grandma to entertain her friends during the week, and woe betide any small boy who was rash enough to interrupt. But on Sundays it was used by all the family, in their best clothes and on their best behaviour. The fact that Grandma had two small rooms at the back enabled her to keep this front room tidy, and herself sane.

The floor of this room was tiled, but I remember it as being mostly covered with colourful rag mats, which Grandma herself had made from scraps left over from dress-making, and from cloth patterns from Grandpa's tailoring business.

What truly fascinated me as a small child in close contact with the surface on which I crawled, was the floor of the back-kitchen which was cobbled. Cobbles were small stones from the river, set in the earth on their edges, so close together that no earth could be seen between them. Those in Grandma's back-kitchen were arranged in a pretty pattern. Outside the back door was a narrow strip of cobbles running along the backs of all the houses, with a roof over it like a verandah. This provided extra working space for such jobs as washing.

Looking at those little houses now I wonder how they managed. There, over a period of 20 years, my grandmother bore 17 children, of whom 4 were still-born, and 6 died in early childhood. Dad has described her picture in his mind, holding a child on her arm, with a foot rocking another in the cradle.

My own earliest recollection of her dates from my crawling days. I see her descending the steep stairs of their house, her white hair piled on top of her head, a tall, straight, imposing figure, with something a little stern about her. In photographs, from youth to old age, the same impression persists. Her magnificent dark eyes gaze out uncompromising and searching. Undoubtedly a strong woman in mind and body. Nor could she have managed her household, brought up her high-spirited children and run the business without that strength.

She married two months after her 18th birthday, my Grandfather being 23. At that time she was the second child and eldest daughter by her father's second marriage, and had already nursed the family through one of the periodic outbreaks of typhoid which swept through the district. She carried water from a spring 3 miles from her home which was believed to be free from contamination, bearing it in large jars or buckets on her head, as in Biblical days. She would carry a sack of wheat on her back like a man, up the steps to the Cenarth Mill to be ground.

She was said to have had the smallest waist, the neatest ankle and the best seat on a horse of any woman in Radnorshire, and I can well believe it, for I inherited a silver-linked belt which she wore even in the days when I remember her. I could wear it only in my youth. She rode side-saddle, of course, and must have been a striking figure as she rode to service at Nantgwyn Chapel. There I presume my grandfather first met her.

Her family, the Prices, were one of the strongest in that church. Her father farmed at Gellidywyll, one of her half-brothers at Nantgwyn and another at Allt Llwyd. (Her father had 9 surviving children by his first marriage, and 8 by his second.) There may have been opposition from her family towards her marriage at first, mainly because she must have seemed irreplaceable at home, but perhaps also there may have been some reluctance to see her marry a tailor. For, craftsman though he was, there was undoubtedly a social and financial gap between them in the eyes of the world. But throughout their marriage the bond with her family remained strong, and their love for my grand-father was obvious.

Indeed he was a most lovable man. Rather short and slim, and very active (He would jump a five-barred gate, cross-legged, tailor-fashion, and could out-run almost anyone in the neighbourhood) he was best loved for his sense of humour and his musical talent. He was one of a family of nine brothers and two sisters. His father, a tailor, died when Grandpa, the youngest, and hence called Benjamin, was a small boy.

It was his eldest brother, William, 18 years older than Benjamin, who then supported the family by tailoring, and I have heard Grandpa tell how he himself walked with his mother from St. Harmon's over the hills to Merthyr Tydfil to deliver a suit of clothes for a funeral, when he was about 9 years old.

William taught his brothers the trade, and Grandpa in turn worked with his nephew Johnny, William's son, who was only about 3 years younger than himself. Johnny eventually married Grandma's sister Margaret Jane, 10 years her junior, and thus was both cousin and uncle to Dad. Two of Grandpa's brothers, Evan and Edward, emigrated to America and became the pioneer tailors of Pennsylvania.

It was only after his marriage that Grandpa set up a

workshop and invested in a sewing machine (though much of the work was still done by hand.) Until then he and Johnny followed the custom of travelling from farm to farm, staying at each while they completed all the clothing needed by that family for that year. This custom was known, for some mysterious reason, as 'whipping the cat'.

Usually they would be given a room to work in, where they would sit cross-legged on a large table, except when cutting out or pressing with the long-handled flat iron called a 'tailor's goose'. The pattern was marked on the cloth with tailor's chalk, a slim block shaped like a sliver of soap. The thread for buttons and button-holes was waxed by drawing it through the head of a candle, making sure it wasn't scorched.

They were given their food, but payment for the garments made might well have to wait until after the harvest or the wool sales in the autumn. The price for making a suit, including waistcoat, was 12 shillings and sixpence apart from the cost of the material.

At one farm Grandpa and his nephew were given a herring between them for their lunch. After lunch, when they resumed their work, singing as usual, the farmer's wife noticed that the tune they sang was extremely slow, and the words rather strange. She listened outside the door, and heard a dirge, sung to the words:
'Half - a - herring. Half - a - herring,'
and when the time came for the evening meal very little work had been completed. For supper they had ham and eggs, and when they went back to work they stitched to a merry jig, to the words,
'Ham-and-eggs. Ham-and-eggs,'
and their needles flew along. Thus they had set up their own primitive form of Trade Union.

But the brothers were even more famous for their musical gifts than for their tailoring. All of them were able to read music, in the Sol-fa notation, being amongst the earliest in those parts to learn it from Curwen's publications. All of them were singers and conductors. All of them were ardent Baptists.

I rather think these factors would soon have out-weighed any hesitation the Price family may have felt, and they consented to the marriage with a good grace.

5

I have no idea which family, the Joneses or the Prices, first learned to read music, for the gift is widespread through both, but my father assured me that he and his brothers, and of course his sister Margaret Mary, were taught to read music as soon as they could read at all.

In his workshop Grandpa certainly worked hard to support his family, but he was fortunate in that it was possible to do much of his work while busying his mind with other things. The little place became known as '10 Downing Street,' for the political debates which took place there. Grandpa would have the Bible open on one side of him, and Reynold's Newspaper on the other, ready for all comers.

He was a red-hot Liberal in the Radical tradition. Gladstone and then Lloyd George were his heroes, and their portraits adorned his home. Sometimes Grandma, aware that it was possible to offend customers, would remind him that 'A still tongue shows a wise head,' a sentiment with which he would agree, but it was not in his nature to temporise. Not that she would have wished him to do so on any matter of conscience.

Sometimes he would pause in his sewing and light up his pipe. He always smoked Franklin's shag, a very strong tobacco, which he kept in a tin shaped like a powder bowl, with a hinged lid which was worked by a spring. Some of his neighbours borrowed a pipe-ful rather too often, so Grandpa invested in a second box. Inside the lid of one he inscribed the words, 'The World', and inside the other, 'Providence.' When his borrowing friends came round and asked for a bit of baccy he could truthfully reply,

"I'm sorry, but I haven't a bit in the world," opening the appropriate box to prove it.

If some of them asked, suspiciously, "Then how do you manage, Jones?" he would answer,

"Oh, I'm relying on Providence."

A large number of families called Jones lived in the village, so naturally Grandpa was called Jones Tailor, and the children were called Henry Tailor, etc. Dad's nick-name was Orly Tailor, his real name being Orlando.

In their home Grandma ruled supreme. Grandpa never interfered with her discipline, which was strict. She kept a birch-rod

6

above the fire-place, and did not hesitate to use it when necessary. To tell the truth, I think Grandpa would have found it more difficult to do so, apart from the fact that he was usually in his workshop.

Dad said that Grandpa had doted on the children who were born to them in the early years of their marriage. Several of them were still-born, which made those who survived all the more precious. When the twins, Ada and Minnie, were born people said that he was never seen without them either in his arms or on his knees. But sadly they died in their first year. Some years afterwards Matilda, a dear little girl of three, also died. Grandpa took this to heart, and seems to have pondered whether he had perhaps made too much of his children. I cannot help suspecting that the idea might have been implanted by one of the Nonconformist Ministers. At all events, he never showed his affection so openly to any of the children who came afterwards.

But if it was a strict home, it was also a loving one. Indeed these two things went together in those days, especially in those brought up in the Liberal Nonconformist tradition

Another aspect of that same tradition was the importance attached to education. My father belonged to the first generation who received compulsory elementary education. Grandpa had been to a 'Dame School', where he had learned to read, and cope with simple Arithmetic, but he and his brothers seem to have taught themselves and each other the type of accounting needed for business from a kind of handbook, beautifully copied into a hard-covered exercise book by John Jones, one of Grandpa's brothers, in 1852. It makes fascinating reading.[1]

The village school was comparatively new. It was a 'Board' school, founded in accordance with the Education Act of 1870, and not by the Church of England, so as Baptists my grandparents would have thoroughly approved of it. Grandpa was one of the Board of Managers, and had been involved in the appointment of the Headmaster, Mr. Rowbotham, and it was his duty from time to time to visit the school and examine the pupils. At such times his own children had to stand up and address him as 'Sir'.

But his visits were greatly appreciated by all the children, for after he had heard them read and perform in Mental Arithmetic he would test them himself in Music, and he enjoyed this so much that they did too.

Mr. Rowbotham found the family so advanced in reading music that when this lesson came around at the end of an afternoon, he would dismiss whichever of the children was in his class at the moment, to go home early. But this was the only privilege they ever received, and in some ways they were even more in the master's power than other pupils, for it was worse than useless to complain at home of their treatment at school.

The only reply would be, "If you were punished you must have deserved it," and they were lucky if they did not receive further punishment at home.

School and home were committed to each other to such a degree that even when he was grown up Dad could never see Mr. Rowbotham's faults. Of these the chief was the savage way in which he dealt out punishment. He had a heavy hand, and very little mercy. Often he would hit the offender behind the ear. His own children were in no way exempt, and it is commonly believed that he deafened one of his own sons in this way. Frequently he would absent himself from the classroom to visit his home, which adjoined the school. (Rumour has it that he drank, but if so it was kept from Dad's knowledge lest it affect his reverence for the Headmaster, for Drink was a Cardinal Sin.) Upon his return he would pick on the first child who caught his eye, find some fault with his work, and thrash him.

But the one time when my father was severely beaten occurred on a day when Mr. Rowbotham, instead of coming out at the beginning of the afternoon to put the children into lines and march them into school, sent his son to do so while he watched from the window. Now this struck Dad as unfair. Reggie was only a pupil like the rest, so why should he be obeyed? Dad said exactly this, and refused to do as he was told, with the result that he had a real thrashing, and remembered it always as an occasion when he felt unjustly treated.

At first Dad was taught by a young teacher, the one he had injured on his first day. She seems to have been very kind, and rather more enterprising than most in those days, for sometimes she would read poetry to her charges. One poem seems to

8

have 'stuck', for I can hardly think that even then they would have been required to commit to memory so unlikely a subject for Infants or Juniors. That poem was *'Queen Boadicea'* by Cowper, and even in his old age Dad could still recite the opening lines:
'When the British warrior queen,
Bleeding from the Roman rods,
Sought, with an indignant mein,
Counsel of her country's gods,'....

But in the main their education was strictly utilitarian, in keeping with the dictates of the Board of Education. It was the period of the Three R's - Reading, Writing and Arithmetic. Scripture was also important, and in this school at least, some music was taught. Writing was learned from Copy Books, and all Mr. Rowbotham's pupils developed a most beautiful Copper-plate hand. Of the family, Victor, the youngest, excelled in this, but all of them wrote in a manner which was commented on wherever they went.

Composition was also taught in the upper classes, mainly from models in books. Dad remembered two amusing incidents arising from this method. The first concerned an occasion when they had been given a model composition on The Cow. This began with the words:
'The cow is a very useful animal. It gives us milk twice a day.'

The pupils were then told to write a composition on The Horse. One unlucky pupil stuck too closely to the model, and began his composition with the words:
'The horse is a very useful animal. It gives us milk twice a day.'

The other odd result of this practice concerned Dad himself. Somewhere he had found a book with a description of Sheffield, and had learned it by heart. At the end of each year they were required to write a composition as part of their examination. Every year Dad produced his composition on Sheffield, and every year he came first in Composition.

From the gloomy classroom with its windows too high for any child to see out and thus be distracted from his work, and its long forms - benches and desk tops fastened together in rows - the

9

children escaped out into the playground at playtime. One of their favourite games, especially with the boys, was Marbles.

This was played with small glass balls, some of them plain in colour, and obtained from the necks of bottles in which they were used as stoppers, but some of them larger, and magnificently striped in many colours. The latter were known as 'Tors', and the small ones as marbles. A circle was drawn in the dust on the ground, the smaller marbles were placed within it, and the players took it in turns to flick their Tor into the circle. Any marbles which were knocked outside the ring became the property of the successful player. But this comparatively peaceful game often gave way to one which would surely be outlawed from any playground now-a-days. This was Cavalry.

By the time Dad was 6 years old Britain was engaged in the Boer War of 1899 to 1902, and he vividly remembered seeing the Montgomeryshire Yeomanry Cavalry riding through the village on their way to take part in the struggle. He would have been much too young to be aware of his parents' attitude to the war. They were supporters of Lloyd George, who was mobbed and nearly lynched in Birmingham for his opposition to what he considered to be a most unjust conflict. But like all small boys, the Llangurig lads were impressed by the glamour of the cavalry, and ardently patriotic.

Dad remembered some snatches of songs from the period, but, above all, the game they played. One boy would mount on the shoulders of another, his 'horse', and attempt to knock over another boy similarly mounted. It must have resulted in quite severe falls on the stony surface of the yard, but the teachers never intervened.

As soon as Dad was big enough to play Cavalry, he always had the same horse, Davey Pryce Morgan. He was a son of Marged Morgan and her husband William, a miner, and they had arrived from Llawryglyn a few years after Dad started school, to live in the little cottage at the end of Wesley Row. Davey, returning to Llawryglyn on leaving school, became a blacksmith, and achieved notable skill in his trade. When he retired, the Smithy of Llawryglyn was taken to St. Fagan's Folk Museum outside Cardiff, where it can still be seen.

But at this early stage in his life what Davey needed most was a friend. Grandma put it to Dad that he ought to befriend Davey, and Dad agreed. Davey could have found no better champion, for Dad fought all the boys in his class without defeat. But Davey he never fought. They became friends for life, and I remember them in their old age, sitting on either side of our fire, going over old times, or exchanging favourite hymns. For Davey developed a talent for translating some of the most famous Welsh hymns into English verse which fitted the tune to which the Welsh words were usually sung.

This most difficult art impressed and delighted my father, who wanted to keep alive the Welsh tunes even amongst English-speaking congregations.

The question of the Welsh language is an interesting one which continues to arouse strong feelings. I can only describe the situation as it was in this particular village at this crucial period.

Llangurig was Welsh-speaking. My grandparents both came from Radnorshire, only just across the hills, but for some reason Radnorshire lost the Welsh tongue early, and neither of them could speak it. Times were hard, and families were large. It was impossible to find work for all the children in the village. Those who tried to find jobs in the towns discovered that they were at a disadvantage because they could not speak English properly.

When they came to choose a Headmaster the Managers decided that it would be wise to appoint someone who was truly proficient in English. What led Mr. Rowbotham to apply I don't know, for he was a Yorkshireman. And that fact probably was one of the chief reasons for his appointment. This was of course in line with official thinking at that time, but it seems clear that in this case at least it was a local decision.

The results were far-reaching. Many of my father's contemporaries, though they always spoke Welsh at home, never learned to write it with any degree of confidence. And when they grew up and married they were less likely to speak Welsh to their children. The language has not yet died out among the native population of Llangurig, despite the effect of almost exclusively English influences through the Press, etc., and the influx of English-

11

speaking people.

There has been a complete reversal of educational policy in recent years, for the authorities have made it a rule to appoint Welsh-speaking teachers to schools like Llangurig whenever possible, and there are now 16 Primary schools in Montgomeryshire where pupils may be taught through the medium of Welsh. But the effect on Dad's generation must have been traumatic, even though I have never heard of any being punished for speaking Welsh on the playground, as happened in many schools at that time. The necessity of studying every subject in a second language must have made it very difficult for many.

It might seem likely that in these circumstances Dad would never have learned Welsh at all, but this was not so, and for this he had Religion to thank.

The nearest Baptist Chapel was 3 miles away, and there the language was English. But when the children were too young to walk there and back they were taken to the Wesleyan Chapel, almost next door. This was Welsh-speaking, and had a flourishing Sunday School. It was in Sunday School that the majority of the previous generation had learned to read, and now it was the Sunday School teachers who set about teaching the English-speaking children Welsh, and the Welsh speakers to read their native language.

They began with the Welsh alphabet and progressed to a New Testament which was printed with Welsh on one side of the page and English on the other. Whether it was originally intended to aid the teaching of English or Welsh, it served its learners well.

The children had to learn verses in both languages to be recited the following Sunday. On the Saturday their teacher would go to Llanidloes, and there he would buy Brandy Balls, a sweet for which Llanidloes was famous. Those pupils who had learned their verses properly were rewarded with a brandy ball. They were quite large, hard, and minty in flavour, and a dark golden brown in colour. In order to make his last as long as possible Dad used to wrap his handkerchief around it and suck the sweet through it. What Grandma thought of the results upon the hanky he never said.

Welsh was spoken in the village, and so Dad would have

plenty of opportunity to practice. He never, however, had the benefit of any teaching in the ordinary sense in Welsh and consequently had no idea whether he was speaking correctly, and for this reason he hesitated to teach either Eric or myself Welsh. Mum did not speak it. So in spite of Dad's efforts, which enabled him to preach in Welsh in later life, it has not become re-rooted in our family.

Grandmother - Elizabeth Jones.

Grandfather - Benjamin Jones.

Margaret Mary and Henry.

Uncle Evan (left) and Uncle Edward, Grandfather's brothers.
Pioneer tailors of Sharon, Pensylvania.

Chapter 2
Politics, Poaching, and Dad's Escapades

As a young child Dad seems to have been singularly without fear. This fact is borne out not only by his readiness to fight anyone, no matter how much bigger than himself, but by the story he told me of a pastime even more dangerous than those I have already mentioned.

He was a great favourite with Dick, Black Lion, the landlord of the largest public house in the village. Dick had two horses, and would take Dad with him when he took them across the river to their grazing   meadow. Dick would lift Dad and place him in front of himself on one of the horses, leading the other by a bridle. Then, when they were half-way across the river, he would throw Dad from his mount on to the back of the other one. This game went on for a long time before Grandma found out, and put a stop to it.

The lads of the village tended to hang around the Black Lion, because quite often strangers would arrive, and be willing to pay a small tip to any boy who would hold their horses while they refreshed themselves at the inn.   But Dad had a richer source of pocket money. For Dick soon discovered that his little favourite had a beautiful voice, and would take him inside and stand him on the bar, to sing to the guests.

Many of these   in those days would have been gentry, for Llangurig was the home of the Lloyd Verneys of Clochfaen, who actually owned the hotel. Thus it was natural that eventually the Verneys heard about Dad's voice. To Grandma's astonishment, one day she received a visit from Mrs. Verney herself. The lady offered to adopt Dad, and send him to St.Paul's Choir School, and continue his musical education afterwards.

This was truly a remarkable offer, and must have caused Grandpa and Grandma some heart-searching, but in the end they refused. I once asked Dad whether he had ever regretted that they did so, and he emphatically denied this, saying that he would not have wished to have been separated from his brothers and sister, and brought up differently. He added that if anyone had made such

14

an offer concerning either my brother or myself, he, too, would have refused to part with us.

But this was not the only offer that they had received from the Verneys, though the other one reflects rather less well upon that family. In 1891 it had been decided to build a new Post Office in Llangurig. It was to be combined with a shop, as is usual with most village Post Offices, for the salary offered to a village Post Master or Post Mistress would not have been sufficient to live on. Since the shop was to be on Verney land, the Verneys had the right to decide who should be the tenants, and therefore Post Master.

It would have been a great advantage to Grandpa and Grandma if they could have been appointed, so they applied. The reply of the Verneys was that they would be delighted to appoint them, if they would come with their family and attend Llangurig Parish Church. They would have been a great acquisition, for by this time Margaret Mary could play the organ, which she did regularly at Cwmbelan Baptist Church, and the boys would have strengthened the choir. But Grandpa and Grandma refused to compromise their religious convictions. Dad said that Col. Verney showed that he respected Grandpa for his resolution, for whenever he passed him on the road he would always lift his hat, and if the coach was going Grandpa's way he would tell the coachman to offer him a lift.

To me these small courtesies do not make up for the injustice. But Dad clearly did not expect any other attitude from the Verneys. In fact, compared with many other families in their position, the Verneys were quite generous to the village and to their tenants, but the whole episode reflects the period, and links up with the struggle for the Disendowment of the Anglican Church, which was one of the aims of the Liberal Party at that time.

Every year a Tenants' Dinner was held at Clochfaen, and as most of those farmers who were not tenants of the Humphreys Owen family of Glyngynwydd (and GlanSevern in Berriew) were Clochfaen tenants, a large proportion of the local population attended. Consequently, although his parents would not themselves have been involved, many tales of such occasions came to his ears.

One concerns a farmer who attended evey year, although he had not paid his rent for a long time. When it came to the speeches,

Colonel Verney one year said how pleased he was to welcome them all, even though he could not quite understand how one man could bring himself to come, since he had not paid his rent for some years. He mentioned no name, and the farmer in question could have remained anonymous. But to everyone's surprise and amusement, the guilty one rose to his feet and explained that he came to the dinner to make it clear that the farm still belonged to the Colonel, even though he could not pay the rent.

On another occasion, one of the Colonel's friends attended the dinner, and rose to make a speech, during which he said that he would like to have been a farmer, for one had only to rear one good horse, and sell it, and the proceeds would pay the rent for a year. This was too much for one of the tenants, a noted horse breeder.

He replied, "Your lordship ought to try it. I'm telling you, you'll rear ten bad uns before you rear one good un."

But paying the rent was not the only obligation upon a farmer. He had also to pay his tithe to the Church. This appeared particularly unjust to those farmers, and they were many in Wales at this time, who were Nonconformists. They supported their own Ministers, and did not see why they should also be called upon to support the clergy of the Church of England. There were many sad cases of farmers who actually could not afford to do so. In these cases the Church Commissioners were legally entitled to sell the stock of the farm and deduct the tithes from the proceeds.

When such a Tithe Sale was to be held, news would spread throughout the neighbourhood, and the Nonconformist farmers in particular would be sure to turn up. Bidding on the stock would be extremely slow. A cow might be sold for a fraction of its real value. The Commissioners would be lucky to have enough from the sale to meet the tithes. However, after the sale was over, and the hated Commissioners had gone away, those who had purchased the stock at such bargain prices would return the animals to the unfortunate farmer who had been 'sold up.' Public opinion was too strong for any local farmer to take advantage of the system and keep his bargains to himself, and it would be a brave soul who would dare, at the sale itself, to drive up the prices by enthusiastic bidding. Such tactics led the Commissioners' agents to seize goods to the value of the money owed, and take them away to be sold amongst strangers.

In this atmosphere politics and religion became intermingled, and Elections were bitterly contested. Grandpa canvassed support for the Liberal candidate, Stuart Rendel, who first won the seat for the Liberals in 1880 and held it until 1893, and for Humphreys Owen, who held it from 1893 to 1905.[2]

Some time after there had been an Election, one cold winter's day, Mr. Rowbotham told Dad to close the ventilator in the classroom. This was a box with a flap on the inside which, when opened, allowed fresh air to enter through slits on the outside of the wall. Dad stood on the form and tried to close the flap, but found he could not do so. The headmaster shouted at him, and Dad stuck his hand in as far as he could, and encountered an obstruction. So he told the master he thought there was something inside the ventilator.

At first Rowbotham refused to believe him, but then he came and tried it himself. Out of the ventilator he pulled two large handfuls of voting papers. When he had recovered from his surprise he told the class that none of them must ever mention to anyone what they had seen.

The school had been used as a polling station, and Dad often tried to establish in his mind an explanation for what had occurred. The franchise had been extended in 1884, (though even after that it has been calculated that only one sixth of the population had the right to vote.) Could it have been possible that some inexperienced voters had mistaken the ventilator slit for the ballot box? But it was the responsibility of the presiding officer to see to it that the votes found their way into the ballot box. So there is possibly some more sinister explanation, though how the fact that the box had been opened was concealed is a mystery. In any case, the Headmaster's anxiety to be rid of the embarrassing question is understandable.

From time to time feelings of injustice made themselves known in more violent fashion. One grievance was the claim of landowners to the fishing rights in whatever rivers passed through their properties. It is not only in Llangurig that lesser mortals have felt this to be completely unjust. But perhaps the so-called poachers of Llangurig were prepared to take the dispute further than most.

17

This was a generation after the period of the Rebecca Riots, which stemmed originally from protest against tolls by which landowners sought to re-imburse themselves for the upkeep of the roads. These fell heavily on farmers, who would find themselves having to pay for the transport of lime and other materials for the land, for carrying feeding stuff, for taking animals to market, etc. Some of them dressed up to disguise themselves as 'the daughters of Rebecca' whose seed, the Bible says, 'shall possess the gates of their enemies', and took vengeance on the landowners and their henchmen the toll-gate holders by destroying the gates, and often when resisted the toll-houses.

But in Llangurig, the primary cause of indignation at this time was the creation of the River Police, as they were called - actually river bailiffs, employed by the landowners.

One Saturday night it was rumoured that **The Rebecca** would be coming to Rhayader, and from there to Llangurig. Quite a number of local men went to meet these protestors, blackened their faces, and accompanied them to the village. They then went down to the river, and used dynamite to blow quantities of salmon out of the water. They impaled these on the uprights of the railings around the church, poured paraffin over them and set them alight. The stench that greeted the gentry on their way to church on Sunday morning can be imagined.

Now Marged Morgan of the little cottage in Wesley Row had longed for a salmon for a great while, so she asked some of the local poachers to bring her one. They obliged, but, perhaps as a joke, did not kill it. Marged placed the living fish in a large tin bath, and became enthralled with it. She took all her callers out to the back of the cottage to admire it, and would say, "Ain't him beautiful? Look at im spots!"

By now the River Police had arrived in the village, but it is hardly surprising that no-one wanted to take them in as paying guests. They went from house and ended up at Marged Morgan's cottage. Whether she knew at first who they were no-one ever really found out, but she took them in as lodgers. Presumably she had eaten the salmon by this time.

Their presence had one other effect. One of the Llangurig girls fell in love with one of them, and, against all advice, married

18

him. However, although he changed his occupation, his un-popularity was so great that they eventually left the village.

Poaching might be popular, poachers might be heroes to most of the village, but to my grand parents poaching was theft. So, although Dad went with his friends during the dinner hour down to the brook, and although he knew as well as any of them how to tickle trout, and even which stone to look under for a big one, and how to spear salmon with a gaff, these skills were never spoken of at home, and he was deprived of the fruits of them. He told me how they would sometimes catch a big fish, and hide it in the long grass, and hurry back to school. Then, at the end of the afternoon, they would rescue their prize, hack it into chunks, and share them. But someone else had Dad's share, for he dared not take it home.

Apples were easier of course. And Dad knew of a very good apple tree, not far from a farm house. Many a time the farmer had chased him, but never caught him.

He would have been about 7 or 8 at the time of which I speak, and loved to visit Gellidywyll, to see his uncle Evan, Grandma's brother. It was a cold winter's day, with heavy grey clouds, but Dad was wearing his new mackintosh, rather long to allow room for growth, but all the better for that, as it came down well past his knees. As he prepared to set off for home, uncle gave him a large tripod, on which Grandma could set a boiler for cooking or washing outside the back door, - also a nice piece of spare-rib of pork.

Dad set off proudly with this burden, thinking how pleased his Mam would be. But he had not gone far before it began to snow. He was not going along the road, for that would have been much further, but across the fields, and over the hill. The snow blew in his face, everything was soon white and blurred, and darkness came on early. Encumbered by his coat and his burden he stumbled along, and soon realised that the landscape had become unrecognisable. He was lost. He had, in fact, crossed over the wrong hill.

How long he wandered around he didn't know, but eventually he could see a light at the bottom of the slope he was descending. That should mean a house, at least. He staggered on and soon he could see another light coming towards him. - A man was coming to meet him. - But as soon as Dad came near enough to recognise who it was, he tried to turn round and run, for his rescuer

19

was none other than the farmer whose apples he had so often stolen. But he couldn't run, and by this time he could barely stand. The coat finally tripped him up, and he fell. The farmer picked him up and carried him into his own house, where his wife began rubbing his frost-bitten limbs back to life, fed him, and wrapped him in warm blankets to sleep off his ordeal.

Meanwhile Aunt had begun to feel anxious about the lad, walking home through the snow. She told Uncle to saddle the pony and ride over to Llangurig, to see if he had reached home safely. When Uncle arrived, and found that Dad was missing, he and Grandpa set out together, and called on neighbouring farmers to join them in the search. They searched and called for many hours, before returning home.

Of course the farmer who had found Dad eventually walked to the village to tell his parents that he was safe, but by this time Uncle and Grandpa and the others were many miles away. So it wasn't until the early hours of the morning that they returned, exhausted, to hear that Dad was safe. On hearing the news, Grandpa fainted.

Stealing - even apples - was wrong, but perhaps the greatest sin in Grandpa and Grandma's eyes was telling lies. On this point Dad told me a delightful story about his brother Herbert, 3 years older than himself, and his closest companion. On one occasion Herbert, and doubtless Dad, had been down in the village with the other village boys, playing.

Somehow Herbert came to throw a stone which broke the window of the Post Office. When they went home Herbert must have decided that his mother was bound to hear sooner or later, so he said,

"Mam, the window of the Post Office is broken."

"What broke it?" asked Grandma.

"A stone,"replied Herbert.

"And who threw the stone?"

This was followed by a long pause, and then,

"Can't talk now."

For a very long time Herbert wanted a knife, but his parents refused to let him have one, obviously thinking him too young to risk it. Whenever the boys had a half-penny or a penny to spend

20

they would go to the village shop, where the others might buy lemon kelly (sherbett) or liquorice, but Herbert would always ask to have a Lucky Dip in a Bran Tub in which were hidden little packets which might contain a small whistle or other trifle. Rumour had it that one boy, once, had received a knife, so Herbert persevered.

One Christmas morning, he and Dad woke early and began, in the darkness, to examine their stockings which they had hung at the bottom of their bed.

"I've got an orange," said Dad.

"So have I - and I've got an apple too,"said Herbert.

They continued to identify by shape and touch and compare notes for a few minutes, then there came a grunt from Herbert, and then silence. It was many weeks before even Dad, let alone his parents, were informed that Father Christmas had given him a knife!

In the early hours of New Year's Day the boys would get up and set out with a lantern to visit the farms around the village. At each farm they would sing carols before being invited in and given *Calennig* - New Year's Gifts. -These were usually mince pies and a warm drink, plus bright new pennies. (*Calennig* derives from *Dydd Calan* - New Year's Day)

Most of the families in the neighbourhood were large, so there was no shortage of playmates, but the boys were expected to do their chores too.

Margaret Mary was the eldest and the only girl, and when she left the village school she attended Gorn View, a school for young ladies, run by the Misses Jones of Foundry Terrace, Llanidloes, where she improved her piano and organ playing and learned more advanced Arithmetic. Then she was apprenticed to the Misses Evans at the Junction House, Pentre Dulas, (later Mrs. Bennet and Mrs George, and first cousins to the Misses Jones) to learn ladies' tailoring. After this the boys had to tackle their share of whatever jobs Grandma needed done. Maybe this was the reason Dad never could see that some kinds of work were women's work and others men's work. This had a strong bearing on the way he brought up my brother and myself. He was the firmest believer in equality of the sexes I have ever met.

As they grew older each in turn was given the responsibility for attending to the cow, and the pig. These shared a shed, which

21

had to be kept scrupulously clean, and the cow had to be milked, and taken to the river to drink. The pig always insisted on accompanying her to the river, and usually had a wallow in the water. Dad was very fond of the pig, and felt very sad when the time inevitably came for it to be killed. But this did not prevent him from enjoying the ham and bacon which resulted. In any case he knew that they would soon have another one.

These two animals played an important part in securing a healthy diet for the growing family. Fresh meat was bought only on market or fair days in Llanidloes, and although a cart visited the village, selling herrings, the usual stand-by was ham or bacon from the flitches hanging from the beams of the ceiling, which Grandpa, like most of his neighbours, considered 'the best pictures in the house'. There were plenty of vegetables from the garden behind the row of cottages, and potatoes from a row in one of Uncle Evan's fields at Gellidywyll, and the latter did a very fine thing for his sister when he presented her with their first cow. This ensured that they had a supply of fresh milk, but as a family they also loved butter-milk, fresh from the churn, after one of the near-by farmers had finished butter-making. Tea was expensive, and was considered a delicacy.

The children did not think themselves hard done by, for all their friends had to help with the tasks of their families on the farms or elsewhere. But Dad never forgot his embarrassment one Sunday night at Cwmbelan Chapel when he noticed that Mrs. Rowlands who sat opposite them could hardly keep from laughing. Eventually it dawned upon him that there must be something wrong with *him*, so he looked down, and to his horror he realised that he was still wearing the coarse apron, made of sacking, which he had tied around his waist, over his best trousers, before milking.

Dad remembered the old oil (Paraffin) lamps in the workshop and in the house, and the great improvement when Grandma bought the new Tilley lamps which were pumped to provide a reservoir of air. The mantle became white and incandescent and gave out a great deal of heat as well as a brilliant light. But they still made candles or tapers from tallow - mutton fat - using the pith of bull-rushes as a wick. These were considered sufficient for going to bed. So there was no temptation to read in bed. But singing was a different matter. One would strike up a tune, and the others would harmonise till the very rafters seemed to be vibrating.

Though he was no farmer, Grandpa loved sheep, and he kept a few as a hobby. He rented a field on the hill above the house, which his eldest son, Henry, enabled him to buy in later years. But he also had permission to graze or to mow the grass in the field at the end of the Nonconformist cemetery, paying for the hay.

From time to time it would be necessary to move the sheep from the upper field to the cemetery or vice versa. Grandpa would set off past the school and through the village, accompanied by his sheep.

He needed no dog, for the sheep would follow him, knowing he always kept a little corn in his pocket. And I remember him leaning over the gate of the field and calling the sheep, and they all came running. The schoolmaster used to cite Grandpa as an illustration of the parable of The Good Shepherd who, 'Calleth his own sheep by name, and they know his voice, and follow him, but a stranger will they not follow, for they know not the voice of strangers'.

Llangurig School

Grandfather's sheep in Llangurig Cemetery.

Obelisk to Chevalier Lloyd
erected in 1885 by tenants and friends.

Chevalier Lloyd.
By permission of National Library of Wales

Llangurig on Eisteddfod Day June 24th, 1909.

Cwmbelan, Llangurig : The Morris family of blacksmiths, and others.

Chapter 3
The Old Ways - Customs and Beliefs

The Cemetery in which Grandpa grazed his sheep was the Non-conformist Cemetery on the Rhayader Road. The existence of this cemetery has an interesting story behind it. It had been a cause of much resentment among Nonconformists throughout Britain that they could not bury their kinsfolk without the rites being performed by a clergyman of the Church of England, who, of course, would use the words of the Prayer Book. In 1880 the Gladstone Administration passed a Burial Act which allowed Nonconformists to perform burials in the Parish churchyard with their own form of service. But even after this many Non-conformists refused to take advantage of the Act lest they antagonise the local clergyman.

This problem came to a climax in the famous Llanfrothen Burial Case in 1888. In this instance a Nonconformist family had applied for rights of burial in the local churchyard, without, naturally, requesting the Vicar to take part in the service. The funeral set off from the house, but upon arrival at the churchyard they found that the Vicar had locked the gates against them. However, they broke down a portion of the wall, and proceeded with the burial. This led to a Court Case in which they were defended by the young Lloyd George, who won the case, and made a great reputation in the process. Two years later he was elected to Parliament.

Llangurig was spared similar conflict by the generosity of Chevalier Lloyd. The Lloyd family had been the owners of Clochfaen Estate for many generations, but the last of that name to inherit was Jenkyn Lloyd who died in 1766 at Shrewsbury, said to have been poisoned at the instigation of Sir Richard Fowler of Abbey Cwm Hir with whom he had been in conflict over the inheritance of the Abbey Cwm Hir estate. The Clochfaen estate passed to his daughter Sarah, but the house had been burned down in 1760. Sarah married Rev. Thomas Youde, and lived to be 91 years old. On her death her daughter Harriet, now married to Jacob William Hinde, inherited the estate.

Their eldest son, Jacob Youde William Hinde succeeded on his father's death in 1868, and adopted the name and arms of 'Lloyd of Clochfaen'. He had been ordained as an Anglican priest in 1840, and was curate of Llandinam for a time. Later he became a Roman Catholic. In 1870, after he had changed his name to Lloyd, Pope Pius 1X created him a Knight of the Order of St. Gregory, hence his title "Chevalier". After the papal decrees of 1870 he gradually became estranged from the Roman Catholic Church, and tried to give up his papal title, but those who knew him personally persisted in using it, and it is by that title that he is still remembered.

In 1885 the Chevalier gave 1½ acres, 'for a Nonconformist burying ground for the parish of Llangurig, and for no other purpose'.

He stipulated that it should not be consecrated by the Church of England or any other denomination, and that no minister in Holy Orders of the Church of England should be permitted to conduct any burial service therein, nor should the service for the burial of the dead according to the rites of the Church of England be performed therein.

Much time was to pass, and many changes, including the Disendowment and eventual Disestablishment of the Anglican Church in Wales, before the rift between the denominations was healed. In the meantime the Llangurig Nonconformists enjoyed peaceful possession of their small plot, and appointed their Trustees, according to Chevalier Lloyd's Deed of Gift, viz:
3 appointed by Chevalier Lloyd and his heirs,
2 by the Wesleyans, 2 by the Calvinistic
     Methodists,
1 by the Independents, 1 by the Baptists, and, surprisingly,
1 by the Church of England.
The 1898 Receipts declare:
In Hand - 19/3d
April 20th from R.Lloyd, Tyn y fron,
5 shillings for right to use a gravestone
Oct. 21 from Benjamin Jones £3 for hay
               Total £4-4-3d [3]
Grandpa became the Secretary of the Trustees whose meetings were held in his parlour. Perhaps it was for this reason that he was one of

the three men present at the Inquiry of the Charity Commissioners in February 1899, the others being Mr. J.H.Rowbotham and Mr. James Jones (clerk to the parish council)

So, for many, the place of burial and the actual type of burial service changed, but tradition dies hard, especially in rather remote places, and perhaps particularly amongst a people such as the Welsh, whose very survival, together with their language, is testimony to the determination with which they have clung to their own way of doing things.

Certainly in Llangurig funerals continued to be conducted in a way which must owe a great deal to very ancient custom. It is not recorded when coffins came into use, but Dad thought it was rather late, for he had heard that it was only after an occasion on which the winding sheet broke on lowering the body into a grave that the local clergy stipulated that in future a coffin must be used.

The news of the death would be announced in the local places of worship, and possibly in the local paper. Dad never referred to the *messenger*, who in the old days would have been sent around the farms in the neighbourhood, to spread the news, so perhaps this custom had died out by his youth. At all events, relatives would come from far and near, and so would the neighbours. To some degree the numbers would indicate the respect in which the deceased or the family were held, and stories of extremely large funerals were handed down with pride in families.

The body would be laid out in the front parlour, and a short service, or at least a hymn would be performed, with the family inside, and everyone else gathered outside the door. Then the bier (or later, the coffin) would be raised on the shoulders of the men of the family, who would lead the procession to the graveyard. This might, in the case of farmers, be several miles distant, and the burden would be taken over in turn by other relatives and friends. It was no easy task, but it was esteemed an honour to be asked by the family to act as a bearer. In some cases a horse-drawn vehicle would be used.

In the days when everyone used the Churchyard, it was customary to refresh the bearers upon their arrival. The body would be laid down under the lych gate while ale was served to those who needed it. This would be mulled or heated in winter time. But the

Non-conformists disapproved of strong drink, so the custom lapsed among them.

Eric, my brother, was a bearer at Grandpa's funeral in 1943, and Uncle Edgar's in 1953. It is only a short distance from the house to the cemetery, and probably by the latter date, greater distances would have been covered by a motor hearse.

One custom was transferred from the old Churchyard to the new cemetery, and that was the holding of a spade over the grave, into which money called *arian y rhaw* or shovel money was thrown. This was for the parish clerk - or even further back, for masses for the soul of the departed - but in my father's time, as far as the Nonconformist cemetery was concerned, the money was for the bereaved family. This has now been discontinued.

After the funeral a meal would be provided by the family for those who had come from a distance. Non-attendance at the funeral of a relative was considered to be a serious matter, requiring a very good reason, and usually every family in the community would be represented. The same applied to women as to men. It is only of recent years that the 'men only' rule has come to apply to attendance at the cemetery itself, and this is not universal.

Weddings too were a matter for the whole community. Again the special *messenger* who used to take the news around the parish had ceased to be called upon. But that did not mean that the news didn't spread, for of course, the banns had to be called, 3 Sundays running, in the parish church of both the bride and the groom. This did not need to specify the actual date of the wedding itself, but in a village, it would be natural that everybody would know. In the case of the Nonconformists there would be arrangements with the Minister and the Organist.

In the case of a young couple setting up on a farm or small-holding of their own, the delightful Love Plough custom still held good. The neighbouring farmers would plough and sow the land for them, so that the first harvest was assured. Other useful gifts also would be given. Of course these favours would be returned by the couple and their families when the appropriate occasion arose. Consequently it was natural that everyone expected to be welcome at the wedding, if not at the ceremony itself, then at least at the festivities which followed.

The lads of the village would hold a rope across the road as the couple left the church, or alternatively when they left the village, and demand payment before allowing the couple to proceed - a custom still practised.

The festivities were very lively, including dancing and games, though by this period the ancient chase in which the young men pursued the newly weds on horseback had ceased. But despite the comparatively Puritan attitude of the Nonconformists, jollification usually continued all evening, though no longer all night and into the next day.

There was one Llangurig girl of my Dad's generation who went to London to earn her living, and got married there. But she later regretted not her marriage but the fact that it had taken place so far from home, in other words, that she had missed having a Llangurig wedding. Being a very determined young lady, she forbade her parents to tell the minister that she had married, and arranged to get married in Llangurig on her next visit.

Custom and superstition survived in other respects also. The district was noted for its *conjurors*. A conjuror was not a man who pulled rabbits out of a hat, but a *dyn hyspys* - wise man - who claimed to be able to cure people and animals, and to make and unmake spells. There was one in Cwmbelan - Jamesy Morris - and one in Llangurig, at Pant y Beni. The latter was a member of a family in which the secret knowledge had been handed down, for he was descended from Edward Savage of Troed y Lôn, Llangurig, whose grandson was practising in the days of Edward Hamer, the local historian who wrote the Parochial Account of Llangurig in the Journal of the Powysland Club.[4]

Hamer quotes Rev.Edmund Jones in **'Apparitions etc. in Wales'** as stating that the first recorded conjuror who lived in the district was a Sir David Llwyd who lived not far from Ysbytty Ystwyth in the adjoining Cardiganshire parish and appears to have been a 'curate likely of that church, and a physician, but being known to deal in the magic art, he was turned out of the curacy, and obliged to live by practising physic.

'It is thought that he learnt the magic art privately in Oxford in the profane time of Charles the Second, when many vices greatly prevailed.'

Whatever truth there might be in this, people came to Pant y Beni from far afield.

Grandpa and Grandma, as good Baptists, strongly disapproved of and disbelieved in such superstition. But Aunty Mary told me that once, when she was a young girl, she had toothache very badly. The nearest dentist was in Llanidloes, and she would have to wait till Saturday to get there. The pain became unbearable, and one night she slipped out when she believed the rest of the family were asleep, and made her way to Pant y Beni.

The old man reluctantly answered the door, holding up his lantern to gaze at her. When she had explained her problem he looked at her more closely. Then he declared,

"Thee bist one of the Pryces. They don't believe in me. I can't do owt for thee." And with that he firmly closed the door.

Hamer tells an amusing story about old Savage, Troed y Lôn[5]: 'The old man, like other great men, was no hero among his immediate neighbours. He prided himself upon his faculty for detecting thefts and tracing stolen goods. A humorous story is related of the means adopted by a number of young men for destroying the old man's prestige in this respect.

'Watching their opportunity, they entered his house one Sunday morning when no one was within, took down a dried ham that was hanging up, hid it very carefully, and then spread a report that it had been stolen. Of course the news created a sensation, and upon his return Savage at once missed the bacon, and shortly afterwards heard of the visit which had been paid to his house during his absence. He vowed to punish the thieves with the most terrible visitations his art could inflict upon them; horns should grow upon their heads, they should be smitten with blindness in one of their eyes, etc., if they did not immediately restore the pilfered bacon. His threats, however, were uttered in vain, his vaunted books were powerless, the thieves met him with taunts -

"Savage, where's your ham?"

"Who stole your bacon, Savage?"

'The conjuror had met his equals in cunning, for they completely baffled his art for days. His wife was more successful, for in changing the straw beneath the paliasse of their bed she found the missing ham, and in a plaintive voice informed her husband of the discovery.

'The old man, who was consulting his books at the time, cried out exultingly, "Well done the old books, they never failed me yet!"

'After serving his generation in his own peculiar manner, he died in the year 1849, having attained the patriarchal age of ninety years; his wife, who lived to be eighty -five, survived him one year. Both lie buried in Llangurig churchyard, where a head- stone marks their graves.'

Hamer recorded this in 1870. But Grandpa, who married and settled in the village in 1875, told the same tale to Dad as having happened to Griffiths of Pant y Beni, the conjuror of their day. But Griffiths was a son-in-law of the later Savage of Troed y Lôn who had inherited the family secrets, and apparently the local tales also.

Whichever conjuror was alive at the time of the next incident, the principal character was John Pryce of Pant-y-drain, a well-to-do farmer and a patriarchal figure whom I dimly remember. One evening he saw a strange woman dressed in black making her way through the village. As she drew level with him she stopped and enquired the way to the conjuror's house. Pryce, pretending to be the conjuror himself, invited her in to the Black Lion. There he asked the landlady to show them in to the back parlour, and surreptitiously asked her to bring him any large books she had. This she did, and Pryce then ordered a whisky, and began to converse with the woman:

"I can see what your trouble is," he began. "You've lost your husband." - Not a difficult thing to guess, considering how she was dressed. - When the woman had agreed that this was so, he proceeded to tell her that she had probably lost a number of creatures from some mysterious disease.

The woman again agreed.

Next he pretended to consult his books, and then told her in grave tones:"Ah, yes. There's those that wish you ill, but I can help you."

After another whisky, for which his client was expected to pay, he wrote out, with much elaborate precaution of secrecy, some words on a piece of paper. He demanded an envelope from the landlady, inserted the piece of paper, sealed it and gave it to the woman, instructing her to place it, unopened, in the *cratch* above the stall of the animal she was most worried about, and to leave it there for a year and a day. After that she was to open it.

What he had written was,

> *"My Dear Woman,*
> *Read more of your Bible. "*

Inside the message was a £5 note.

The holders of the larger farms, such as John Pryce, were the leaders of the community, Chapel Deacons , Church Wardens, School Managers, Members of the Parish Council, etc., alongside craftsmen like Grandpa. An equally memorable character was James Jones of Llwyn Gwyn, who was Clerk to the Parish Council. Another of his duties was to collect the rates. Once a year he would go around those who had not yet paid, greeting them with the words:

"I be comed for the Rates - That is, if it be convenient."

If it was *not* convenient, James would pay over them rather than bring them officially into arrears. Annually he submitted his account book to the Clerk to the County Council at Welshpool.

On one occasion he had asked the Clerk for a new Account book because the old one was full. The Clerk sent for him and complained that they could not find a book large enough, though Llangurig was far from being the most populous parish.

"The trouble is," said the Clerk, "that you never cross anybody off. Half the people in your book have been dead for years."

"They may be dead to thee," replied Jones, "They binna dead to me. I'll tell thee what the *real* trouble is. My name be James Jones, Llwyn Gwyn, not John Pryce, Pant-drain. I be wrong *colour* for thee."(John Pryce was a Tory, and James Jones a Liberal.)

In later years, when Grandpa and Grandma were growing old, Uncle Edgar, the next to youngest son, and the only one who was still a bachelor, remained home to look after them. Jones Llwyn Gwyn decided to retire, and to get Uncle appointed in his place, thinking that the small payments for his duties wouldn't come amiss. Having succeeded in his plan, he came to Uncle to give him some advice.

"Thee'lt have to have a Committee," he said, referring to the Parish Council. "Thee must send the names to Welshpool. But dunna thee let any of them know they're on it, or they'll get ideas

31

above themselves. And dunna thee *ever* call a meeting, if thee canst help it. But if theest bound to, thee mind to be thy own Chairman."

The very idea of mild-mannered, humble Uncle Edgar carrying on in this way is comical, but clearly Jones had got away with it for years.

The Lewises and later the Turners of Bryn Cylla were another prominent family, loyal Wesleyan Methodists, whose son, Eddie, would have become a Minister but for the fact that he developed Tuberculosis, and died young. Uncle Edgar for many years courted their daughter Lizzie Anne, and after Grandpa's death they were married. Her sister, Ada, told me that her grandfather, Edward Lewis, nick-named Justice Bryn Cylla, was one of three men who had saved the village from being submerged by a dam.

It seems that those who wanted to erect the dam had submitted a Bill to Parliament, in which they had stated that the valley was almost uninhabited. The Bill had reached the House of Lords when the villagers became aware of their danger. Justice and two companions went to Westminster and proved to their Lordships that there was a Church, several Chapels, a small school, shops, two public houses, and a number of village houses. The Bill was defeated. But there were other villages in Wales which were not so lucky.

Memories of this incident may have served to encourage their near neighbours of Nantgwyn, Tylwch, and the rest of the Dulas valley when they were threatened by a similar scheme in the 1970s. It was a little more difficult to make the case for the community understandable to English people, because, unlike Llangurig, there is no obvious centre. The nearest Church is at St Harmons, and the other elements are scattered about. In this respect it is much more typically Welsh, for the Welsh, right back to the days of Giraldus Cambrensis, have not generally lived in villages of the English pattern. But the community is a real and a close one, and in spite of the temptation of considerable sums in compensation most of them rallied and fought the case to a triumphant conclusion. It was from this area that both Grandpa and Grandma came, so the struggle concerned Dad deeply.

Llangurig - building of Ebenezer C.M. Chapel 1903-4.

Llangurig Parish Church Interior.

Clochfaen Tenants' Dinner. Line-up outside Black Lion. Pre - 1888.   *John Thomas.*
By permison of the National Library of Wales.

Llangurig. The rebuilt Black Lion Hotel

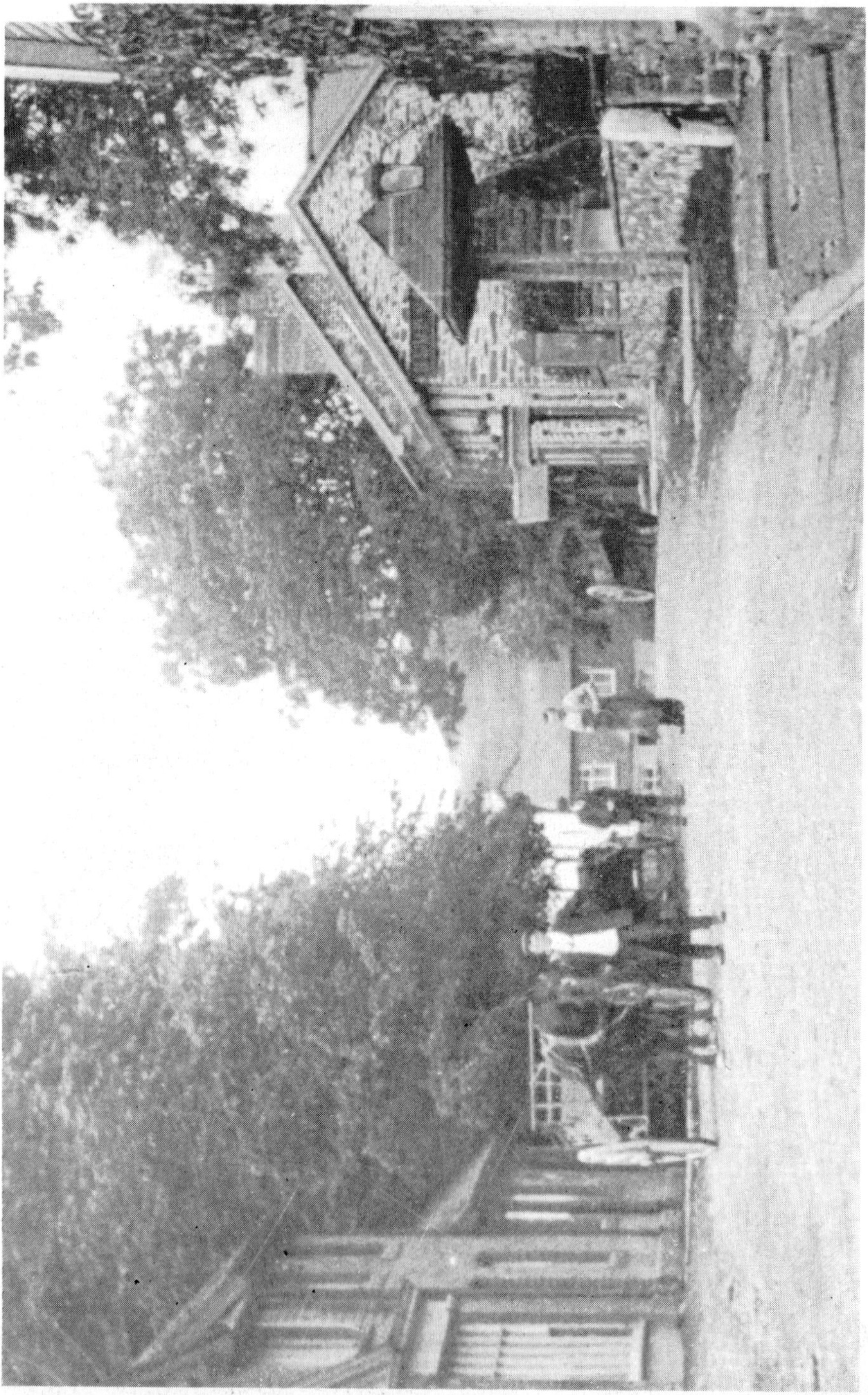

Shearing at Ystradolwyn Farm, Cwmbelan (for details see Appendix).

Great Oak Street, Llanidloes. Cattle Fair c. 1890
By John Thomas with permission of the National Library of Wales.

Davey Pryce Morgan, Llawryglyn. Shoeing a horse.

By permission of the Welsh Folk Museum, St. Fagan's, Cardiff where Llawryglyn Smithy may still be seen.

Chapter 4
Change in the Family and in the Village

Next door to Grandpa and Grandma lived an elderly lady called Mrs. Williams. If the boys became too noisy she would take up her poker and tap on the back of her fireplace, which of course backed on to Grandma's. That was usually enough to quell them, but if it didn't, Grandma would intervene. Dad remembered that when Mrs. Williams was ill Marged Morgan who lived in the cottage above the Chapel came to look after her. Marged could be heard 'chorusing' Mrs. Williams, referring to her as 'an old besom', but energetically scrubbing her floor out of the goodness of her heart at the same time. From Mrs. Williams the Dumsdays of Wallasey, still close family friends, are descended.

During Dad's years at school there were changes in the family. Mary completed her training as a tailoress by the Misses Evans, and for a while she was employed as a Sewing teacher at the local school, and also did some private dressmaking.

Henry left home, and began work as an Insurance Agent for the Pearl Assurance Company in Llandrindod. His Uncle, Edward Price, Grandma's brother, was an Insurance Agent in Rhayader. Uncle Edward was married to a school mistress, whose earnings, more reliable than his, supported the family. She kept him like a gentleman, as Dad used to say. Henry married Miss Minnie Brick, and they had one daughter, Megan. Like all the family he was very musical, became well known as a conductor, and had great success at Eisteddfodau.

Sometime during his school days Dad had a bad fall and was taken to see Doctor Morris in Llanidloes. The surgery was at 44 Long Bridge Street, the very house where Dad was to make his home in years to come. The Doctor found that he had broken his collar bone, and he set it for him. When it was time to remove the plaster, he rewarded Dad for his courage in standing the pain so well.

Many of Dad's clearest memories were connected with Cwmbelan Baptist Chapel. Grandpa was the conductor or

Precentor for many years, and until her marriage Mary was the organist. The harmonium was very old, and before she went away to South Wales she collected enough money to buy a new one. It is still in use.

Naturally all the family were involved in events such as the Anniversary. A few years ago one of my cousins showed me a faded, yellowing cutting from the local newspaper, with an account of Cwmbelan Anniversary, including a Recitation by Orlando Jones, aged 5 years. But most frequently as he grew up Dad sang solos, duets, etc. The family could have held an Anniversary on their own, for they were all talented, like my cousin Daisy's family after them.

But they were not alone. Most of the families were large, there was little in the way of entertainment, and many took great pleasure in developing their skills in singing and reciting. There were classes in Tonic Sol-fa, which enabled most of them to read music, and considerable rivalry arose between the various denominations in the area as to who could produce the best choir.

Grandpa was involved also in the Association meetings of the Baptist Churches in Montgomeryshire and Radnorshire. This is still known as **The Old Association**, and was one of the earliest in Wales. There were times when affairs didn't go smoothly, and Grandpa on one occasion, after Dad had left home, confided in him when he came on holiday, "If you want to be happy in a Church, keep out of office." But this was not his usual frame of mind. He was an ardent believer in the Baptist view, and in later life he pleaded with Dad to become involved in the wider affairs of the Denomination, because he feared that their distinctive witness would eventually die out, swallowed up by the larger denominations. The tide of religious controversy has ebbed since Grandpa's day, though how much is due to increasing tolerance and how much to apathy is debatable.

There was little sign of apathy in Cwmbelan Baptist Church, in those days, but they had an earnest desire for even greater enthusiasm. A great religious Revival was sweeping Wales, having begun through the ministry of Evan Roberts in 1904. He was a young Methodist who began as a lay preacher.

The little church at Cwmbelan held a number of Prayer

Meetings to pray for the gift of Revival to be granted to them. There were among them men and women of deep Christian piety, well read in the Scriptures and in works of theology. But there were also those with a more limited understanding. One of these, a very fervent woman, prayed one night that the Revival would come up from South Wales, "Past Capel Calvin, and Capel Bethel, Llanidloes (both Methodist) and come to Capel Baptist Cwmbelan *first.*" One night the prayers had continued rather long, and one little girl found it necessary to go outside to relieve herself. To her astonishment, the sky was lit up from the horizon with great beams which seemed to sweep across the sky. With her imagination full of the 'tongues of fire' for which the church had been praying, she dashed back inside and shouted out, "Come quick and see. The Revival has come!" Unfortunately the great beams of light had a more mundane explanation. - There was a large Pleasure Fair which that night had set up on the Gro, Llanidloes, and the lights would be clearly visible from Cwmbelan.

The period during which Dad grew up was a great one for the development of music in the Nonconformist denominations. In particular there were many fine composers of hymn tunes. Together with the spread of the ability to read music, this gave rise to the desire of congregations to improve the musical quality of their worship. This was the impulse behind the establishment of Choral Festivals all over Wales. Our own Montgomeryshire and Radnorshire Association established theirs in 1888, and among the members of the Founding Committee were Grandpa, and Grandma's brothers. This Festival has recently held its Centenary and is still doing good work, though the numbers attending, and the churches represented have decreased over the years.

Eisteddfodau were also spreading, and a number of people in Llangurig, encouraged by Chevalier Lloyd, decided in 1881 to hold their own, entitled **Eisteddfod Gadeiriol Clochfaen** (Clochfaen Chair Eisteddfod, indicating that a Chair would be awarded for the best poem.) A photograph of the village taken during the 1909 Eisteddfod shows the large crowd assembled.

Grandpa was on the committee from the beginning, and they must have raised enough money to give sizeable prizes, because some of the best choirs and soloists in Wales came to compete. If this makes the competitors sound mercenary, I should explain that they would have paid their own transport costs, that they were amateurs, and that the larger the prize, and the stronger the competition the greater the prestige of winning.

For the main solo competitions the prize was usually a silver cup, often accompanied by a sum of money. Good soloists would travel about the country from one Eisteddfod to another, some of them to such an extent that they were derided as 'pot hunters,' for it was expected that having won at a number of smaller meetings, an artist would then withdraw and compete only at the National or Semi-National Eisteddfodau. Llangurig didn't quite rank as one of these, unlike Llandrindod, but for a small village it attracted a remarkable range of talent.

Such Eisteddfodau gave local people the chance to hear singing and reciting of a high standard, and enabled them to appreciate the finer points through the adjudications. They also encouraged composers and poets.

I believe Wales is the only European nation in modern times to award its highest honour to a poet, as did the ancient Greeks.

It still amazes me that at this time there were in many Welsh villages men of humble occupation, farm labourers, carpenters and the like, who could write poetry not only in the so-called free metres, which are as restrictive as formal metric verse in English, but also in *cynghanedd*, the strict Welsh metres with their elaborate system of cross alliteration.

The Festivals and Eisteddfodau were special occasions. Holidays, in our modern sense of a time to go away and enjoy ourselves, were almost unknown, but each of the children in turn, as they reached a certain age, were invited to stay in Neath with Uncle Dick, Grandpa's brother, who was a gardener. Dad described the house as having a brook running before the front door, with a little bridge across it, and ducks swimming in the water.

Uncle seems to have been a placid man, under the control of his more forceful wife. She would offer him something at the table, asking him if he wanted it. When he replied,

"Yes please,"

she would wait until he amended it to,

"Yes please, my dear."

36

While they stayed with him Uncle would tell them of certain pranks that Grandpa had taken part in when he was a boy. They were pledged to secrecy and each thought he or she was the only one to be so favoured.

The holiday seems to have been a delightful experience. But it would have been accompanied by a little home-sickness, for it was for each their first time away from home. Mary apparently threw herself into Grandpa's arms on her return, crying, "I haven't had dinner since I left." Enquiry revealed that what she had been deprived of was potatoes. Dad too never really freed himself from the impression that dinner had to include potatoes !

We are accustomed to thinking of our own age as one of great change, but the times in which Dad grew up were almost equally so. The village to which Grandpa brought Grandma changed beyond recognition during a very short period.

As yet the smith had no need to worry. The village boys still gathered to watch, sometimes to help blow up the furnace, sometimes to lay straws on the anvil while the smith's back was turned, hoping for a minor explosion when he laid the hot iron across it, and always for gossip. The art of the blacksmith, like tailoring, was passed down in families. In Llangurig the blacksmith was then David Rees. In Llanidloes and Cwmbelan the Morris family carried on the trade for many generations.

For a while it must have seemed as if the railway revolution would sweep away Llangurig smithy like so many others. The Llanidloes to Newtown Railway was opened in 1859, and the line was cut and laid to Llangurig. It was intended to join the Llanidloes to Builth line, hence the house called **The Junction** built below Cwmbelan. One train actually ran to the village, in February 1863, carrying coal and lime. But funds ran out, and the line closed. Its track lay opposite Wesley Row, where the Council houses now stand, and can still be traced beyond them.

Grandpa, as soon as he could afford it, kept a pony and trap, in which smart turnout he drove to town. While they attended to business the pony would be placed in the stable belonging to one of the public houses, and the trap parked in the yard behind.

But although the smithy remained, much of the village was rebuilt. In 1877 Chevalier Lloyd of Clochfaen conveyed a piece of

37

land to the trustees of the Calvinistic Methodist Chapel, on which they built a row of cottages called the Green Cottages. During the last 10 years of his life the Chevalier spent a great deal of effort and expense on the renovation of the parish church, under the guidance of Sir Gilbert Scott, the leading architect of the Gothic Revival movement.[6]

In 1885 the Obelisk was erected in the village 'by his tenants and friends as a mark of gratitude and esteem for his unbounded liberality'.

When he died in 1887 the estate was inherited by his niece, Harriet Julia Morforwyn Verney (née Hinde), and her husband, Colonel Hope Verney, who took the surname Lloyd-Verney in compliance with the Chevalier's will. She and her husband continued building.

At Clochfaen itself a farmhouse and cottages, built in 1877, were remodelled, and the barn enlarged to form a Tenants' Hall for the twice yearly rent taking and celebration for the tenants and other guests. The Black Lion Inn was rebuilt as a Hotel in 1888, its walls hung with tiles, and the Post Office in the same style in 1891. In 1894 Mrs. Verney gave the land for the Church House.[7]

When Mary started to attend school in 1883 she was entered in the Register as the daughter of 'Benjamin Jones - tailor - of Pen-y-capel', but in 1902 the Morgan family are registered as living in 'Wesley Row'. Probably the terrace took this name when the cottages were renovated in 1894.

In 1898 the fountain was erected in the middle of the village to commemorate Colonel Lloyd Verney who had died in 1896, and the completion of the village's piped water supply.

Ebenezer, the new Calvinistic Methodist Chapel was built alongside the Green Cottages in 1904 to be a replacement for Penybont Chapel which was proving too small as a result of the Religious Revival. Mrs. Lloyd Verney is said to have disliked the fact that it could be seen from Clochfaen Hall, and therefore planted a row of fir trees behind the chapel to screen it. Dad used to say that she had unintentionally done the Methodists a favour, because the trees when grown provided a wind-screen as well.

Where the old chapel had stood Mrs. Verney built the Police Station and Penybont Cottage in 1907. These buildings, together with the Black Lion Hotel, the Post Office and the Fountain, all in the style of the Arts and Crafts Movement, gave the village an unusual and attractive character.

Just outside the village, between the Llanidloes and Rhayader roads, the Verneys made an artificial pool, Tan-y-llwyn Lake, large enough for boating. Apparently in later years this was destroyed by the excessive overflow caused by a violent thunderstorm. The pool is mentioned in the literature produced by the Lloyd-Verneys who hoped to make Llangurig a tourist centre.

(Perhaps this hope was shared by their son, Harry Lloyd Verney and his wife Lady Joan Verney, for when they inherited in 1913 they immediately set about remodelling Clochfaen Hall, with the help of the architect William Arthur Smith Benson.)

Dad's sister Mary married William Davies, (Willie) eldest son of Mr. Davies, Bwlch-y-Garreg, Cwmbelan, and soon afterwards they left for South Wales, and settled in Bargoed. South Wales at this time was booming in the sense that the coal industry was growing rapidly. Many of the people employed in the mines came from Mid Wales, where times were hard. It was very difficult to obtain land to rent, and even employment as a farm labourer wasn't easy to find.

Some took work as miners for the major part of the year, but returned home for the Harvest. Some families kept their smallholdings going by this method.

But the growth of centres of population provided other opportunities. Willie became an Agent of the Pearl Assurance Co. and he and Mary studied Book keeping together. He did well and rose to more responsible positions, eventually becoming District Manager at Pontypool.

Gwilym began work at Red House Farm, Llanidloes, and later Herbert was apprenticed to S.P.Davies, Ironmonger, of Long Bridge St., Llanidloes. The shop stood where the Lowcost Supermarket is now. I remember all the wooden drawers beautifully lettered with the names of the various nails, screws etc. that they contained, and being told that my Uncle had done all the lettering.

Grandpa kept the Apprenticeship Agreement document, and I remember Dad showing it to me. The terms seemed harsh, though I expect they were typical of that time. Grandpa had to promise to keep Herbert respectably dressed, and he actually paid S.P.Davies for the training. I believe the apprenticeship was to last 7 years.

Some time after Mary had married and gone to South Wales, Grandma was taken seriously ill, and Mary came home to look after her. This was to be the pattern whenever there was trouble. For this I greatly admire Willie. He never complained. On this occasion, it was quite a long time before Grandma could face solid food. When eventually she thought she would try it, Mary cooked something she was sure Grandma would enjoy, and Dad asked for the privilege of taking it upstairs.

"Eat it all, Mam. It'll do you good." he said. But when he went up again and brought the tray downstairs, he had a very long face. Mary asked him why.

"She did eat it all," he replied.

But in truth Dad nearly worshipped his Mam. There came a time when it was Grandpa who was very ill. Just how ill came home to Dad when he saw Grandma in tears. She asked him to go down the village to buy something from the little shop which she thought might help. On his way back, Dad knelt down on the road and prayed for his father's recovery.

He didn't, of course, say anything about this to Grandma, though she might have wondered why he was rather long coming back. But eventually she noticed the mud on his knees, and questioned him. When he told her, she hugged him. I believe it was then that he discovered that one can pray without kneeling down.

Sometime during this period Uncle Evan (Jones), one of Grandpa's two brothers who had emigrated to America, came home on a visit. Both brothers were doing well, and Evan brought with him a new system of pattern-making which Grandpa was quick to pick up. His account of the greater opportunities impressed the boys, especially Gwilym. He either went with Uncle Evan when he returned, or followed shortly afterwards. He settled in Ohio, at first farming. In one of his early letters home he described how he had been sent out into the fields to supervise a group of Negro workers. He didn't know their names, and began by shouting out, "Hey! You! Nigger! " Very soon he found himself surrounded by a group of threatening black faces. One of the other white workers had to rescue him, and explain that 'nigger' was an insult, and make peace.

40

Another surprise arose from his longing for swedes. These were a favourite vegetable with all the family, especially when mashed with potatoes to make 'stump'. Grandpa sent out some seed which Uncle Gwilym planted, but the swedes which resulted were too hot to be eaten. Obviously the soil in which they were grown made a great difference to the flavour.

Later Gwilym found employment at the steel works at Sharon, in common with many other Welshmen. It was very hard work, but probably better paid than similar work in South Wales. He worked hard and saved hard.

At the time when Gwilym went out Dad was about to leave school, and was sorely tempted to emigrate with them. Uncle Evan obviously realised he was too young, but he promised Dad that he would eventually send over the fare for him to join them. This had not been discussed in front of Grandma.

Hanbury Road Baptist Chapel, Bargoed c. 1908.

The Bargoed Branch of the Tredegar Co-operative Society c. 1908.

A mission gallery. By permission of Dangaard Library.

Chapter 5
Dad leaves Home and learns a Trade

Dad left school on his 14th birthday and shortly afterwards set off for South Wales to join Mary in Bargoed. Grandpa had made him a smart suit with knickerbockers and a Norfolk jacket, which he wore with long socks and stout boots. They came to Llanidloes station and Dad boarded the train. Grandpa put him and his trunk in charge of the guard. Dad had no idea how far it was to Bargoed, and as soon as they came to a station he would get up and find the guard to ask him, "Is this Bargoed?"

The guard soon got tired of this performance, and eventually took Dad into the Guard's Van, where he pointed out a large box labelled 'Bargoed.' "See that?" he said. "Well you sit on that box, and when we come to Bargoed I'll throw that out, and you after it."

They were slow, the trains that ran on the Mid- Wales line of the GWR (The Great Western, otherwise known as God's Wonderful Railway), and the Guard's van, at the end of the train swung from side to side and rattled. It would have been draughty too, and uncomfortable, surrounded by mail bags, wooden boxes of anything from vegetables to kippers, and bundles of newspapers which the guard would fling out at the Halts where the train didn't stop unless you had previously asked the guard to arrange with the driver to do so.

But it would also have been exciting to anyone who had rarely experienced any form of transport other than a horse. I don't suppose Dad thought the train was slow! The clouds of steam, the chugging of the wheels, the long whistle (so different from the silly squeak of the modern diesel) would have added to the excitement. And although he was going away from home, out into the world to earn his living, he was fortunate in that he would be living with his beloved sister, Margaret Mary. So he wouldn't have been very nervous, though he must have wondered what kind of place Bargoed was.

I don't know whether Mary had described it at all. I only know that when Mum first visited it she was shatteringly disappointed. She told me that from the way Dad spoke of it she had felt it must be little short of Paradise. But that, of course, was coloured by all the nostalgia for lost youth.

The reality must have hit Dad almost at once. For Bargoed was a coal mining valley, with long grey terraces of miners' houses lining the hillsides, one below the other, and the mine with its winding gear at the bottom. The air was filthy with coal dust and smoke, for the miners were allowed coal for their own use as part of their wages, but naturally it would be the poorest quality coal which produced clouds of smoke and very little heat.

High above the valley rose the moorlands, but these too had been polluted. Here were the slag heaps of waste from the mines, flat-topped and sloping-sided. From them ran filthy streams where the trout had once lived, and the few sheep which tried to find a living by nibbling the thin grass soon became as scraggy as the pasture itself, and took to raiding the dustbins in the valley below.

But among the mean houses a few shops had sprung up, at first just the front room of an ordinary house, but gradually enlarged, and then replaced by a proper shop front. The first of these were the shops provided by the mine owners, known as the 'truck' shops, from which the miners were compelled to buy, at inflated prices, because the owners paid part of their wages in vouchers to be exchanged for goods. There had been a struggle against this, and by the time Dad went down South it had been won, but wages were very low.

There were now a few private traders, a Co-operative Society shop, and one large Ladies' and Gents' Outfitters shop known as **The Emporium**. Dad's description of this last reminds me of Mog Edwards' shop in Dylan Thomas' **Under Milk Wood**, 'where the change hummed on the wires'. There was a system of wires running above the heads of the assistants, carrying cylindrical boxes. When a sale was made the assistant would reach up and unscrew the end of one of the boxes, place the money and the bill inside the cylinder, rescrew the end and pull the wire. This would operate a spring and the cylinder would glide along the wire to the till, where the cashier would remove the money and the bill, and put the change and receipt back into the little box which would be sent on its return journey. - Much more fun than our modern electronic check-outs !

But Dad was apprenticed to a much less sophisticated business, a small private grocer's, where he worked nearly all the hours God sent for half a crown a week and a pound of cherry cake.- Half a crown was two shillings and sixpence in old money, 22½p. in decimal currency. It is true that it would buy much more then than now. But considering the hours Dad worked it really was a very poor return. They accepted it because Dad was only an apprentice. As for the cherry cake, Dad said it tasted like sawdust, and they never ate it.

It was Dad's job to sweep and scrub the floor, polish the counters and the brass scales and weights, and help to unpack and check the goods. Sugar came in hard cone-shaped blocks known as 'sugar loaves'. Their shape has given a name to several Welsh hills. The sugar had to be scraped and crushed, then weighed and packed. This was quite skilled work. Dad taught several grocers in Llanidloes how to pack so that no string was needed for tying, and he always packed his takings for the bank in this way, until the paper bags were replaced by plastic. He also learned to twist a length of grease-proofed paper into a funnel which would hold a half-penny-worth of vinegar. In fact almost everything they sold had to be divided into smaller portions, weighed and packed.

Many of their customers would bring in an order which Dad was expected to deliver. For this purpose he was provided with a small hand truck. The deliveries were usually done after the shop closed, and this entailed pushing the truck up the steep slope to the top end of the valley, and up the sides to the top terraces. There he would often find that the living rooms of the lodging-houses were filled with men sleeping on the floors, many of them drunk. He had to pick his way over them, fearful of disturbing them, to find the woman in charge and make his delivery. When he had finished, usually after night-fall, he would sit on his truck and career down the cobbled streets to the bottom of the valley. In later life he wondered how he had escaped without a broken neck!

After a few months Grandpa came to visit Mary, and to see how Dad was getting on. He was very upset when he found the hours Dad was working, in particular on a Saturday night, when the last deliveries sometimes took place in the early hours of Sunday morning. He decided that Dad must find another job. But very shortly afterwards Dad turned up one morning to find the door of the shop locked. There was a man outside who told him that the bailiffs were in, which meant that his boss had gone bankrupt.

Dad had not been paid for the previous few weeks. He went round to the back of the shop, and found that his little truck still stood in its usual place, so he took it, regarding it as the tools of his trade, and bearing in mind that he would be the last of the creditors to be paid.

He had seen a notice up in the window of the Co-operative Shop, advertising a job for a boy. So, with his truck he went along and applied. To his relief they engaged him. And so began a period during which he was known as 'Orly the Co-op'. Despite his old-fashioned clothes, which the other boys laughed at when he first arrived, he seems to have been popular, both with his contemporaries and with older people, and he did well in his job.

Soon he was allowed to use one of the Co-op vans to deliver, and stood in line with the others to stock up with bread. But he found that his van had more than its fair share of yesterday's bread, and learned to stand up for himself and his customers.

It was at about this time that Dad asked Grandpa to buy him a pony. She eventually arrived on the train, and Dad was extremely proud of her. Her name was Peggy, and he spent many hours grooming her. Like most ponies and horses she soon learned the round Dad followed day after day, and while he was delivering at one house, she would slowly walk on to the next. One day a woman was passing, and seeing the pony moving while unattended she thought Peggy was running away. She shouted at her and lifted her apron and waved it in front of her to make her stop. This seriously frightened Peggy who bolted along the street. She might have caused an accident but for a soldier who was passing. This man had lost an arm, but he bravely seized the pony's bridle and hung on until she calmed down. By the time Dad caught up with them she was quiet.

After a while Dad was given a chance to serve behind the counter. But he first had to unlearn some tricks which his ex-boss had taught him. The old man used to place a rasher of bacon under the scale on which he placed the rashers to be weighed. This would, of course, reduce the amount needed to make the scales level. He explained to Dad that he had to pay for all the wrapping paper used in the shop, and this was the only way in which he could recoup the cost. The last customer to buy bacon from a particular joint would have the spare rasher, and Dad thought that customer was lucky! The manager of the Co-op was horrified when he found Dad doing this.

But the Co-op had its own peculiarities. One, which was fundamental to the whole system on which the Co-operative Societies were based, was that at the end of each quarter each customer's order book was totalled, and a percentage, based on how profitable the store had been during that quarter, would be distributed to each customer according to how much each had spent at the store. Each customer was also a share-holder and this was therefore a distribution of profits or dividend, and was universally known as 'The Divi'.

If a customer had bought a large quantity of goods Dad would fetch a big box from the back of the shop and pack the goods in it. One woman came in one day to complain that he never put down the price of the box on her book. He explained that as she was a good customer he didn't think it was fair to charge her for an empty box. But she replied that if he didn't charge her she would lose her 'Divi' on the box!

The share-holders elected a committee, and Dad soon found out who they were, for they and their wives expected extra attention. The Secretary of the Society was in control over the manager and all the staff. Where there was a good Secretary and a few knowledgeable members on the committee the system worked well, even though there was plenty of cause for friction between the Manager and the Secretary. But where this was not the case it was easy for the Manager to cheat the share-holders.

Dad wasn't paid much by the Co-op, when he joined the staff, but he gave Mary some money for his keep, and of course some had to be set aside for Collection in Chapel. There wasn't much left for spending - perhaps a few pennies a week.

One thing Dad really enjoyed was jelly, which they sometimes had for tea on a Sunday. But as Mary had three children, Ewart, Wilfred and Glyn, the jelly had to be shared between six. Dad decided that for once he would like to have a jelly for himself.

So he saved up his pennies and bought one. He borrowed a dish from the larder, melted the jelly, and hid it under the sofa in the front room, thinking it would be safe there for at least long enough for it to set.

The first thing he did when he came in from work was to examine his jelly. But to his surprise it hadn't set. He left it until the next day, but it was still liquid. On the third day he thought that perhaps there had been something wrong with his preparation, so he asked Mary how much water one needed to melt a jelly.

"One pint", she said.

"That's funny," he said, and then he told her about his jelly.

"Oh, it set all right," she said. "We all enjoyed it, but I left a bit for you, and added more water. That's why it didn't set. I wanted you to learn not to be selfish!"

Dad was more like a son than a brother to Mary, and all his life he looked up to her. One day when he had been living with her for some time, they were talking about their Uncles in America, when Dad said that he didn't think much of Uncle Evan. Mary asked him why, and he said that Uncle had promised to send him the fare to emigrate, but he hadn't done so.

Mary replied, "Oh, but he did. I found the letter one morning, and I couldn't understand why he should be writing to you on your own, so I opened it, and there was the money for the fare. I knew it would be the end of Mam if another of her children went abroad, so I sent it back and told him we wouldn't let you go."

It was while he worked at the Co-op that Dad began to know the other young people of the town. He was now working more reasonable hours, and could spend some of his time as he pleased, though his sister kept a watchful eye on him. She encouraged Dad to study book-keeping at the Evening Institute, and of course the chapel played a very important part in their lives. In those shabby streets of cottages put up by the mine owners for their workers, the chapels, paid for largely by the members themselves, (mostly workers) stood out like palaces. They were taller than all the other buildings, for they had galleries, and most of them had classical frontages and pillared porches. Inside they were furnished with pitch pine, beautifully varnished, and most of them had good organs.

47

The chapel they attended in Bargoed, Hanbury Road Baptist Church, was a most impressive building which had recently been completed. It had large school rooms at the back in which a number of activities took place during the week. The minister at the time was Rev. Harry Edwards, a fine preacher and scholar, who had a young family about Dad's age. One of his sons, Oscar, became Dad's best friend.

But his greatest joy, then and always, was music, especially choral singing, and his ambition was to join the Bargoed Male Voice Choir. This was already very famous, having won at the National Eisteddfod and many other competitions. You couldn't just decide to join such a choir. You had to take a test to see if you were good enough. Dad put his name down, and the day came for him to take his test. He managed the sight-reading with ease. Then the conductor, from the piano, put him through voice exercises to establish the range of his voice. When he had finished he looked at Dad and said, "You're a Chinese puzzle!"

Dad's heart sank, and he thought he had failed the test. But the conductor asked him what he most wanted to be. Did he, for instance, want to be a soloist?

Greatly daring, Dad replied, "I'd rather become a conductor like you, sir."

The conductor, T.R.W.Lewis, was delighted. He said, "I will teach you all I know, if you will sing in any part of my choir as I ask you. You have the widest range I have ever heard, from bottom Bass to top Tenor, and you're a marvellous reader. You can help my choir to learn any piece. But it will spoil your voice for solo work. Do you mind that?"

Dad didn't mind that at all, and as a result he retained his wonderful range into old age. He could lead any part of his choir when they were learning pieces. And if his voice wasn't good enough for the National it was still very strong and mellow.

The accompanist of the choir was Master Sidney Northcote, then about 10 years old. This remarkable young musician later became Dr. Sidney Northcote, Professor at the Royal Academy of Music, but at that time his parents went with him to all the performances.

The valleys of South Wales at this time have been described

as a melting pot, because people from so many different backgrounds came there, drawn by the availability of work, or by business opportunities. Among them were Irish people, some of them originally navvies or navigators, the men who dug the canals which, preceding the railways, opened up the country to trade.

They were Roman Catholic, and so were the Italians who established fish and chip shops, ice-cream parlours and cafés. These, unlike any run by Welsh people, were open on Sundays, and presented a temptation to the local youths, after service. Dad, Oscar, and I am sure many others used to go to one of these on a Sunday evening after Chapel, to drink coffee and play cards. Mary probably didn't know this. She would have considered it to be Sabbath breaking, and seriously wrong.

Dad was widening his experience in other ways too. About this time a Theatrical Company toured the valleys with the play **The Way of the Cross**, and Dad went to see it and was deeply moved by this depiction of the sufferings of the early Christians in Rome.

Shortly afterwards Rev. Harry Edwards preached an evening sermon on Esther the Beautiful Queen in which the action of Esther in risking her life for her people was likened to the sacrifice of Jesus on the Cross. Dad had arranged to meet Oscar and his other friends as usual in the café after the service, but when the last hymn ended he felt he simply could not go. So he stayed to the 'after meeting' of the members, at which the question was always asked whether any one present had decided to accept the Lord Jesus Christ as their personal Saviour. Dad indicated that he had decided, (by remaining seated while all the existing members stood) and was invited to join the Minister in the vestry at the close of the meeting.

To his surprise he found that Oscar too was waiting to see his father. At first each was a little indignant because the other had not warned his friend of his intentions, but they soon accepted that both had acted on the spur of the moment.

Rev. Edwards was a bit disconcerted too, when he asked Dad to what he attributed his conversion, expecting to hear that it was one of his sermons, but Dad, while admitting that the sermon on Esther had made a great impression, said that the chief influence had been the play, **The Way of the Cross**. The minister explained that many actors and actresses lived lives which were scandalous, and indicated that he would prefer Dad not to visit the theatre in future.

Immediately after his talk with his two young converts Rev. Edwards was due to hold his usual Sunday Evening Open-air Service in the main street of Bargoed, and he asked both of them to go with him and take part. Dad was frightened, as he had never spoken in public before, but Rev. Edwards assured him that all would be well. Dad often described how when he was called upon to give his testimony he kicked the ground with the heel of his boot until he blurted out the words, "Something has happened to me tonight."

He never knew what he said after that, but his minister told him that he would never again speak so effectively as then, 'red hot' from his conversion. It was the initiation into a life-time of service.

Soon afterwards he and Oscar were baptised, at the age of 16, and made members of the church.

Dad joined the chapel choir, and was persuaded to take charge of the Band of Hope. This was a children's organisation dedicated to the fight against strong drink. The members were encouraged to sign the pledge that they would never drink alcohol. In later years there was a branch in Llanidloes, and Dad encouraged both of us to join, but when it came to our signing the pledge he would not allow us to do so, declaring that we were not old enough to know our own minds. His troubles in Bargoed, however, were of a much more practical kind. He arrived one evening, perhaps a bit late, to find that the children who were supposed to wait outside had gone in and were playing 'Firemen' with water from the ends of the radiators. In future he made sure that he had the key.

The churches at that time had good reason to oppose the breweries, for they were opening public houses all over South Wales, often at the approach to the pits, so that many men went in for a drink on their way home, and never came out until they had drunk all their pay, with disastrous effects on their families. Also the abuse of alcohol contributed to many mining accidents. Rev. Edwards attended every Magistrates' Licensing Session in his area, to protest at the granting of further licences. But it did not need any such influence to make Dad a teetotaller. He was brought up to be one.

Hanbury Road Baptist Chapel at this time needed a piano, and the agents of Keith Prowse, who supplied instruments, made an unusual offer to the deacons. They would supply a piano at a much reduced price, if for a year previously they could place in the church a series of instruments which were for sale. One Sunday Dad noticed a particularly fine piano was there, and he fell in love with its tone. During the following week he went so far as to enquire about its history, and learned that it had belonged to the musician Caradoc Davies, who had been paying for it by instalments. When he had first received it from the makers he had sent it back because he said the bass was too weak, and they had trebly strung the bass to satisfy him.

Unfortunately he had failed to keep up the payments. The firm said they would be willing to sell the piano for the amount of debt outstanding. Dad made an agreement with them to pay it off at the rate of 2/6 per week. He must have had a rise from the Co-op to have been able to do this, and probably Willie would have been guarantor, but it was a remarkable step for a young man of sixteen. The piano remained with Mary until Dad married, and both Ewart and Wilfred learned to play on it. Dad gave it to Mum as a wedding present, and both Eric and I learned to play on it, but Dad never did. He always seemed to have been too busy singing and conducting.

Miner, with winding gear in background. *By permission of Bargoed Library.*

List of mining disasters, 1837-1927. *By permission of Bargoed Library.*

Chapter 6
Upheaval - The Riots, a New Career, The War.

After a while the Co-operative Society sent Dad to another of their branches, at Maes-y-Cwmmer, further down the Rhymney Valley. This meant that he had to go into lodgings, but at the same time he was now appointed an assistant, and his pay was increased. (Eventually his salary rose to £1 per week).

He joined the local Baptist Church, just at the time when they needed a conductor, or Precentor as it was usually called. Sixteen was very young for such a responsibility, but he was well recommended. One of the deacons wanted to give him some good advice before he took up his duties. He was a gentleman more used to the English tradition than to Welsh enthusiasm, and he begged Dad to promise him that he would not indulge in "all these repetitions." - When carried away with enthusiasm a Welsh congregation might repeat the last verse or the chorus of a hymn several times. - Dad, however, would give no such promise, on the grounds that he could not interfere with the workings of the Holy Spirit. In the course of the next three years the Society moved Dad from one department to another so that he received training in all aspects of the retail trade, including butchery, boots and shoes and clothing, as well as groceries. This experience stood him in good stead in later years, and he always felt that if one line of trade failed him he could turn to another. He was a natural optimist, as I suppose all successful salesmen are. In the grocery department he learned an alphabetical list of the goods for sale, and sometimes when confronted by a customer who couldn't think what else it was she wanted, he would recite this at great speed, confusing her more than ever, but always producing a great laugh.

He worked in several branches in the valleys, but he went home to Mary as often as possible. It was on one such visit that he found himself caught up in the outbreak known as the Tonypandy Riot, although it was far more widespread than that name suggests.

The trouble began with a dispute over the piece-work rates

offered at the Naval Colliery, Penygraig, in the Rhondda Valley, which the miners said would not produce a living wage. On September 1st 1910, the owners locked out 800 men. The dispute spread and by the beginning of November there were 3,000 men on strike throughout the coalfield, and their families were experiencing hardship. Their wives had exhausted both money and credit and many of the smaller shops had already closed. There was little food in those which remained open, since the owners could not pay their suppliers.

The centre of the struggle was the Rhondda valley, and Tonypandy in particular, but it is worth remembering that the men of the Powell Duffryn Colliery, Bargoed, had set up World records of production. On December 10th, 1908, they produced 3,462 tons for a 10 hour shift. This was followed by 4,020 tons on April 23rd, 1909.

On October 29th 1909 there was an explosion at the Darran Colliery, Bargoed, in which 27 men, including 5 rescuers, lost their lives. This was only 8 years after the Senghenhydd disaster, when 81 men were killed. Small wonder they felt their work and their lives were undervalued.

On this particular day a large crowd had gathered in Bargoed, in an angry mood, and stones began to fly. The shopkeepers who were open hastily put up their shutters and locked their doors. One solitary man, Shibko, the pawnbroker, stood on his doorstep with his rifle and defied the rioters. Then the rumour went round that there was butter in the Co-op, and they gathered outside the shop. The doors were locked, but the new plate-glass windows wouldn't last long.

By chance Dad was in the street. He went round behind the store, and found the back door open. When he went in he discovered the manager cowering under the counter. Dad, though only 17, persuaded him to get up and open the doors. He argued that they would be no defence against a mob. He found a soap box and placed it in the doorway and stood on it. Most of those in the crowd recognised him, and there was a moment of something like silence.

Dad asked them what they wanted, and they told him that they had heard that there was butter in the shop. He said that he doubted it.

Then he said,"You don't have to believe me. You appoint someone to search, and I'll appoint someone too." He noticed an ex-soldier with one arm, and said,"This man has given his arm for his country. He shall be my choice."

They agreed, and appointed a miner to go with him. When they had searched the shop they reported that there was no butter, only a little margarine and some dripping. Dad told them that if they would form a queue they should each have a few ounces of the fat until it was all gone. Then he went in and helped his old boss to serve what was now an orderly queue of customers. They bought other goods as well, most of them of course on credit. But at least there was no more violence that night.

A few days later soldiers marched through the valleys with fixed bayonets. This was something for which Winston Churchill, then Home Secretary, was blamed, and for which the South Wales miners never forgave him.

Dad saw the episode through very different eyes from the miners. He was genuinely afraid of mob violence, and relieved when order had been restored. It made a lasting impression on him and coloured his political views. Not that he agreed with the coal-owners, but he believed the Miners' Federation could have bought the collieries, and that this would have been a better use for their money than strike pay.[8]

He never considered his action to have been very brave. He simply did what seemed best at the time, which was typical of his impulsive nature.

In 1911 when he was 18, Dad began a new career, as an agent for the Pearl Assurance Company. He was probably influenced by the progress Willie had already made with that company. Also there was a streak of independence in him which meant that he took satisfaction from building up his own 'book' of customers, on which his commission was based. He was still an employee, but there was more scope for his enterprise.

He no longer needed Peggy, so she was sent back to Llangurig, where she grazed on Grandpa's field. Perhaps she pulled the trap when Grandma went to town.

Grandpa, however, had a new means of transport - a

Penny-farthing bicycle, the first in the parish. He mastered the art of mounting - quite a feat with that enormous front wheel - balancing and riding, and one Saturday he set off to ride to Llanidloes. On the way he overtook a woman driving a trap. Her pony, startled at this strange sight, reared up. Grandpa wobbled and swerved, then turned the bicycle into the hedge and jumped, cross-legged, landing in the woman's lap."Tailor, the Devil is in thee!" she cried.

Gwilym, who came over on a visit, was much impressed by 'Pa's Wheel' as he called it. Like most young emigrants he had acquired an American accent as quickly as possible and wasn't loth to use it in Llangurig. But he had thoughtfully brought his father an American scythe, which was lighter and easier to use than the traditional Welsh one. Grandpa demonstrated it to Dad when he went home, and Dad insisted on trying it out. Unfortunately he had little experience of using a scythe, and drove the point into the ground, thus bending the blade.

An insurance agent sees many aspects of humanity which are not revealed to others. Added to which, the agents themselves are worthy of study. This was a period when the companies were building up their clientele. They didn't pay their agents much in salary, so the pressure was on them to earn commission. They were expected to find a certain amount of new business every month. But at the same time they had to keep a wary eye open for those prospective customers who were not telling the truth. One woman tried to pass herself off as her sister in whose name she was taking out a policy. Dad found out that the sister was a cripple who was not expected to live long.

Another very different case was a religious man who wanted to know what would happen if the Second Coming of Christ took place and he was raised from the dead. Would his children have to repay the money received on his Life Insurance Policy? Dad had to write to Head Office in London on this one. The reply came back in which the Company stated quite seriously that they would not demand repayment, but that if he should die *after* that, they would not pay out a second time.

The problem of collecting the premiums, usually weekly, was something they shared with rent and rate collectors and others.

Whenever employment is uncertain, debt becomes a widespread blight on families and communities. Dad saw both sides of the problem. - The families sinking into a morass from which they could find no way out, the hire-purchase firms repossessing furniture, families turned out onto the street for rent arrears. - On the other hand there were shopkeepers who could not obtain payment of the debts owing to them, and consequently couldn't pay their own suppliers.

In Dad's case it was vital that he get payment of his premiums. It was forbidden to pay over a client. If they defaulted they would eventually lose the money they had already paid in. Dad could use this fact to persuade them to continue, but if the policy lapsed there was nothing he could do, and it would count against him too.

Then there were the sad occasions when he had to call on a family and pay out because the father had been killed in a mining accident. He described how, when the mine hooter sounded other than at the beginning or end of a shift, everyone would stop what they were doing, and the women would wrap their shawls around their heads and go to the pit head to wait for news. The dread settled on the whole community. Any miners not on that shift would volunteer to go down to try to rescue those who might be trapped below, even though they knew they were risking their own lives. The waiting might go on for many hours before the men in charge of the winding gear would have the heart-rending task of bringing up the cages not of their live comrades but of their mangled bodies.

Such would be the case at disasters involving many lives. But there were many 'smaller' accidents in which 'only' one or two were injured or killed. No less a disaster for them of course. Then someone would try to warn the wife before the little procession came to her door, carrying her husband.

For this reason the miners' wives had a dread of the tramp of boots at any unusual time of day.

One agent was a North Walian whose English was very 'lumpy', as Dad would say. He turned up on one woman's doorstep with the query, "Wass your husband in the pit?"

The woman changed colour, and the agent, to re-assure her,

said, "Not you frighten! 'Surance it is!", with the result that the woman fainted.

Dad's progress at work was rapid. Within a year of being appointed an agent in Bargoed he was promoted to Assistant Superintendent in the same town. The National Health Insurance Act had just come into force and was operated through the Insurance Companies. Dad had to master the details of the Act and instruct his agents in the working of it.

Willie was promoted to Superintendent, and moved to Pontypool. Dad's Superintendent at this time was a man called Mr. Crowther. - A dour man who went through his morning post like a knife through butter by giving each query from Head Office one of three replies: "Yes", "No", or "Receiving attention". By 9.30 a.m. he would be out on the road with one or other of his agents, except on Thursday, Accounts Day. Perhaps it was this cavalier treatment of his superiors which told against him when it came to promotion - or was it the other way round? There was a District Manager, Mr. Abel, who had started working for the Company at the same time as Mr.Crowther. Naturally Crowther was not best pleased at his colleague's promotion over his head.

Mr. Abel was a more affable person, though Dad was much in awe of both of them. Actually the laconic style was to some degree typical of the Company itself. When a man left their employ and applied for a reference, all they would supply would be a statement that 'We have nothing against this man.' - All very well, if the recipient realised that this, in Company terms, was the height of praise.

The Pearl Assurance Company met its obligations in all the disasters, but it was to be faced with a much greater test, when the 1914-1918 War broke out. None of the men had been insured against the chances of life and death in the trenches or in the front line, but the Company paid out on every life insured. Fortunately their resources held out. The agents were very well aware of the importance of keeping up the inflow of new business, and the existing premiums, to counterbalance the outflow to the families of the bereaved.

Dad was 21 when war was declared, and Herbert was 25 and working in Hitchin, Hertfordshire. Both volunteered to join the

Royal Welsh Fusiliers. Herbert was accepted, did his training and was promoted to Corporal. But the Pearl Assurance Company appealed to retain Dad's services. This was granted, and they immediately instructed him to take over the management of Ebw Vale as Assistant District Manager, with two Assistants and 37 agents under his supervision.

Meanwhile the ranks of the Pearl's agents were being thinned because so many volunteered, and later many were called up. Dad found himself doing more and more work, for all those not yet in the Forces felt that they had to support those at the front by ensuring that their policies didn't lapse, and that the books of the agents who were fighting were not neglected. Added to this there was a drive to sell War Bonds, which Lloyd George described as 'silver bullets'. Dad won a gold medal for selling the largest number of such bonds in his area - £1,000 in small sums. He worked through all weathers, often when he should have been in bed.

Then Herbert came home on leave, and Dad was fortunate to be able to take a holiday. Naturally Herbert wanted to visit as many of the family as possible, including Grandpa's nephew Johnny and his wife, Grandma's sister, Margaret Jane, who then lived with their daughter Annie near Rhayader, in Radnorshire. They would have cycled there.

Uncle Johnny was not only a tailor. Like all his brothers he was a singer and a conductor of choirs. Annie had a beautiful contralto voice and became a very well known singer. Henry (also a conductor) came over from Llandrindod, and together they had a most enjoyable evening singing, playing cards, telling stories etc. Eventually, Henry decided he had better go home, but Herbert and Dad weren't ready. Henry however was concerned about his mother, waiting at home, and probably getting anxious, so he persuaded them to leave. Dad and Herbert waved him goodbye and went a little way towards Llangurig, but then turned to each other and said with one voice, "Let's go back." And so they did. Henry however had his suspicions, and he too turned back, to find them once more sitting by the fire. This time they were ashamed, and gave him their word they really would go straight home.

It was a small incident, but it lived in Dad's mind because it was Herbert's last leave. On 9th October 1917 he was killed in

58

action in France. He was 28 years old. He and Dad had always been very close, and the shock was dreadful.

Not long afterwards Dad's great friend Oscar was drowned. I don't know any details. Dad never talked about it, but he had a photo of them together and they looked like brothers.

I believe these two great losses were partly responsible for the breakdown in health which followed.

In August 1918 Dad received his call-up papers and once more the company prepared to lodge an appeal. But in the meantime, when he went for his Medical examination he was astonished to be rejected. He was told there was something wrong with his lungs. He had been working while he had pleurisy, going out in all weathers, and this would, of course, have caused damage, but he started to worry that he had Tuberculosis, which was such a scourge in those days. He developed insomnia and lost a lot of weight. Eventually he was admitted to the Sanatorium at Talgarth.

Before the development of inoculation the only treatment for the disease was by a strict regime regulating rest and activity on a graduated schedule. The patients lived in cabins with open windows in what was virtually an isolation hospital. Those who sneaked down to the village to snatch a glass of beer were severely reprimanded, and if they repeated the offence they were sent home.

While he was at Talgarth he became friendly with a young man called David Bateman who was a poet. David had hoped to become a vicar, and had begun to study with this aim, but he found he could not conscientiously assent to the 39 Articles, in particular the one which declares that Jesus ascended bodily into Heaven. He simply couldn't believe that 'bones and all' ascended and were now in Heaven. And so the Church lost one who was a very sincere Christian. He sent Dad and Mum a Bible as a wedding present, and each year we used to receive at Christmas a slim volume of poems, or a specially composed Christmas poem.

Dad was never diagnosed as being tubercular, but as he went through the stages of the treatment he recovered his spirits, and organised concerts among the patients. He didn't, however, overcome his insomnia, and when he had completed the treatment the doctors thought that perhaps a return to his native air would help. Llangurig air is naturally much healthier than that of the South

Wales valleys, especially at that period. But he continued to suffer, rising in the night, or staying up, hoping to tire himself, and wandering about the village in the early hours.

One Sunday morning he was watching people going to Church when he noticed two young ladies whom he didn't know. One was tall and stately with black hair and rosy cheeks, but it was the other one who captured Dad's attention. She was small and slim with masses of soft brown hair, piled up as was the fashion, and surmounted by a broad-brimmed black straw hat, with a big red rose on the front. Dad only saw her back, on that first Sunday, but it was enough.

Herbert. Corporal B. H. Pryce Jones, Royal Fusiliers.
Killed in Action on October 9th, 1917.

My father, Orlando Jones (on right) with his friend Oscar Edwards.

My mother's family.

Back row: Joe, Sally, Tom. Middle row: Grandfather (William Jones) and Grandmother (Margaret)

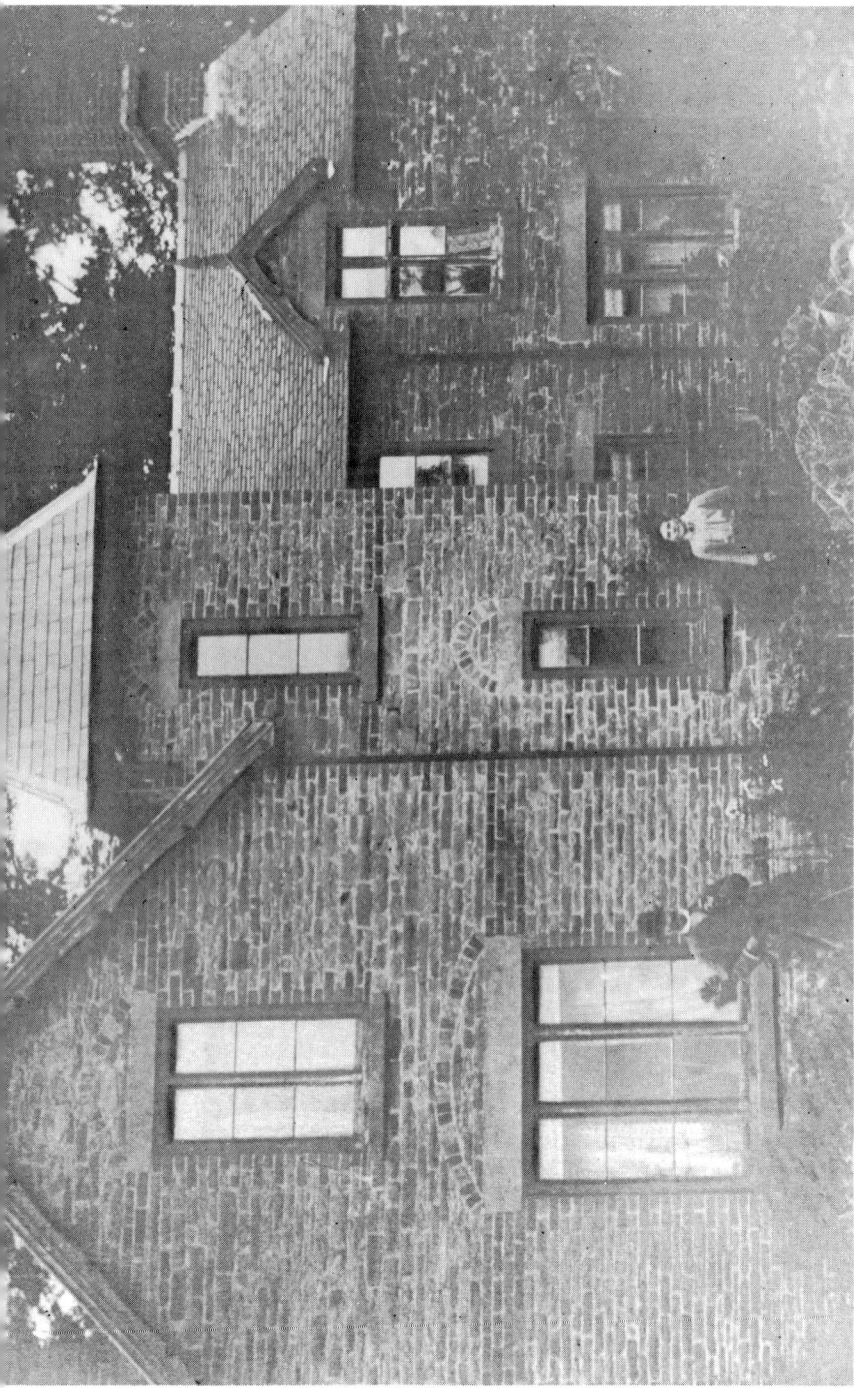

Peny Byrwydd Castle, Caereinion. My mother's home.

Part Two   Mum

Chapter 7
Growing up on the Farm and at School

I have a photograph of Mum aged about 6, with her long hair beneath a Breton straw hat. She is wearing a dress with a sailor collar and a full skirt, long socks and little boots. I'm sure that's what little girls wore for best in those days. I can picture her hatless and in a less formal dress playing outside her home, throwing a stick to the dog, or playing tug of war with him. Despite being one of a large family she was a rather lonely child, because there was a gap of six years between the twins, Maggie and Katie, and Mum. There had been a little boy in between, whose name was Edward, but he died very young. Mum never knew him, but she used to imagine what it would be like to have him as a playmate.

The youngest child isn't always spoilt, and Mum certainly wasn't. There was far too much work to be done on the farm. Also Katie was always weak and in need of extra care. But as long as Sally, the eldest was at home Mum wasn't in any danger of neglect. When she was a small baby, Sally, who was then 16, nursed her a good deal, and probably that was when the bond between them was forged.

It was very natural. After Sally came the two boys, Joel and Tom. Then the twins, ten years younger than her, who seemed not to need any other company. Then, to everyone's surprise, came this little girl. Grandma wasn't well after the birth, and so Sally took over for a while. She was very cross that her wishes weren't taken into account in the naming of the child. She hated her own name, Sarah Ann, considering it to be very old-fashioned. To her intense annoyance Mum was christened Mary Jane - equally old-fashioned. So she informed the family that though the baby might be christened Mary Jane, she wasn't going to be *called* that. Sally called her May, and soon everyone else did too. I didn't even know Mum's name wasn't May until I went to College.

I was about 16 when I realised that Mum hadn't been born at Pen y Byrwydd, near Castle Caereinion. In fact she was born in Llanidloes Parish, at Bryn Coch, but the family moved when she was two years old, and she had no recollection of her first home.

I learned later that all the other children had gone to school in Llanidloes, and Sally had gone to 'Finishing School' at Gorn View to be taught by the Misses Jones: Miss Polly, Miss Lizzie and Miss Louie, the last two of whom were accomplished musicians. Sally had no great gift for music, but she learned a little, and was also taught drawing, pen painting in coloured wax on such things as cushion covers and fire screens, embroidery, and of course, 'how to be a young lady'. It didn't really satisfy her. She would have preferred a more academic education. She must have been a student there about two years after Dad's sister, Mary, who benefitted so much from the Mathematics teaching, but Sally had less occasion to build on this foundation.

The house still stands, though the surroundings have altered. It is the last house of the row leading to what was then the Millses' Iron and Brass Foundry. At the back there were two school rooms. On the opposite side of the road was the garden, with a rose arbour, where the young ladies used to sit between lessons. If one of the men from the Foundry should happen to pass they were supposed to keep their eyes down and not look at him.

Sally would have left Gorn View, and the boys would have left school when they moved to Pen y Byrwydd. Those were the days before cattle trucks, and the stock had to be walked all the way, a distance of over 30 miles.

Pen-y-Byrwydd, which Grandpa rented from Humphreys Owen of Glan-Severn, was a couple of miles from the village of Castle Caereinion, built on rising ground just below the Byrwydd Hill from whose top parts of 5 Counties (the old Counties) can be seen. It is a grey stone house decorated around the windows in red brick, with an imposing tower in the middle, part of what seems to be an extension of a simpler farmhouse. The view from the house is magnificent, but the situation would be bleak in winter.

In front of the house Grandma had her garden of flowers and herbs. Mum and her sisters remembered that she grew a fuschia bush and trained it in the shape of a chair, with a cushion of nasturtiums in the centre. The herbs were for medicinal as well as culinary uses, for she knew many old-fashioned remedies, and like Grandma Llangurig was often called on for help and advice. Behind the house lay the orchard of apple, pear and plum trees. The apples were stored in the attics on slatted shelves which Joel made. The pears were made into Perry, and elderbloom and elderberry and other fruits were made into wines. On one occasion Grandma decided to throw out the old perry which had become rather sour in order to re-use the bottles, so she poured it on the midden. Shortly afterwards the hens were seen to be reeling about the farm yard like sheep with the gid.

There was a small Congregational (Independent) Chapel in the neighbourhood, and Grandpa, who had been a Sunday School teacher at the Congregational Chapel in Llanidloes, began to attend. But there was some kind of dispute going on and one Sunday when he came home he told Grandma that he wanted to worship in peace, so he decided to go to the local Parish Church. Grandma had been brought up in the Parish Church at St Harmon's so she would have been quite happy about this. All the children were eventually confirmed as members of the Church.

'Castle' as it was generally called was a small village, but the church is rather large, and set in a circular churchyard. It is said that this indicates an ancient foundation, possibly built on a site already sacred before the coming of Christianity. The remains of the Castle have disappeared, but there are several houses in the area which belonged to the gentry, and the land of the valley is rich. Castle Caereinion, like Manafon and other churches in this neighbourhood, has always had a Rector rather than a Vicar. The Rectory still stands in the village, a pleasant house in its own grounds, with a lawn before it which was used in Mum's day for croquet.

Mum's father, like Dad's, was an ardent Liberal, but more active still. He canvassed at election times for Humphreys Owen, and later for David Davies, and spoke on platforms at political meetings. Like many farmers he was inclined to forget all about time on such occasions. He seems to have left much of the responsibility for the work of the farm to Grandma, and in this he was not unusual for that time. Like many other farmers' wives, she worked indoors and out, especially at shearing and harvest.

Grandpa was popular and quick-witted, also quick-tempered. He had a squarish figure, sandy hair, blue eyes and a moustache. He would have gone shooting with Humphreys Owen, as well as keeping down rabbits and pigeons on Pen y Byrwydd. The work of the farm was, of course, very much more labour-intensive than now-a-days. All ploughing and harrowing was done with horses, reaping was hard labour with the scythe, and the mechanical thresher was only just coming into use. They needed farm labourers in addition to the three men of the family, and these lived in the village, but had their meals at the farm.

At harvest time, when even more help was needed, the women also worked in the fields, and neighbour helped neighbour to defeat the uncertain weather. They kept dairy cattle too, and Grandma made butter for sale in Welshpool Market on Mondays, together with eggs from her beloved hens. There was weekly baking and a great deal of heavy washing and ironing - most underclothes and the men's working shirts were made of Welsh flannel. Always the house-work had to give way to the necessity of having the meal on the table as soon as the men came in.

The journey to Welshpool market was usually by pony and trap, but sometimes Grandma had to go on the brake, a kind of cart on which the seats were placed along the sides, facing each other. She really hated this. She was inwardly very reserved, and the merry gossip around her often made her cringe, but she had to disguise her feelings.

At the market she got a good price for her butter and eggs, and spent the proceeds on household shopping. This was the usual pattern, but there was an occasion when it gave rise to an argument between her and Grandpa. He declared that it was a waste of money to keep hens. He bought the corn to feed them, and received nothing in return. So Grandma decided that in future she would keep an account. The bills for the corn were set aside, to be paid out of the money from the market. Meanwhile, the bills for the groceries would be Grandpa's responsibility. He was soon glad to revert to the old ways.

Welshpool was, as it still is, the administrative centre of Montgomeryshire, with an imposing Town Hall, on the ground floor of which the market is held. The building dates from 1796, and its size was partly dictated by the fact that the Court of Great Sessions - now the Assizes - took place there. The upper floor was also used for the large flannel market which was held on Thursdays. Another important element in the prosperity of the town is the Smithfield, said to have been the largest in Europe, which is held on Mondays, regardless of Coronations, Funerals, Jubilees or

64

any other National events.

The town is over-shadowed by Powis Castle, home of the Earl of Powis, so it became quite naturally the social centre for the gentry of the area, many of whom had town houses in Welshpool, some of which still add distinction and variety to the main streets. But the back streets were until recent years crowded with very inadequate houses along little alleys which could be shut off at night - hence the name 'shuts' used for them by the local people.

Although this was where Grandma sold her produce and did much of her shopping, she also visited the shops in Llanfair Caereinion. This is a much smaller town than Welshpool, but it has the enviable nick-name of 'Shining Llanfair'. There are different explanations for this name, one being that this was the first town in the county to install electric street lighting. The name, however, goes back further than that would suggest, and is possibly due to the habit of the townspeople of white-washing their houses. This was the custom in the countryside, most farms being white-washed to the very gate posts every year. Llanfair had few of the rather grand red brick houses, and fewer still in stone, so the old fashion persisted, the town was bright and clean, and whenever a place had been cleaned and polished well it was said to be 'shining like Llanfair.'

The contrast between the two towns lay deeper than mere appearances. Welshpool was - and still is - Conservative. Llanfair was, and remains, Liberal. On one occasion Mum had gone to Llanfair to do some shopping for Grandma, wearing a little blue costume. The last thing in her mind was the fact that there was an election approaching. Suddenly she was set upon by a gang of children who began to throw stones, calling her a Tory and many uglier names. Fortunately the noise drew the attention of a draper who knew Mum and her family well. He pulled her into the shop and hastily bundled up a length of red ribbon which he pinned to her shoulder, so that she could go home safely.

When I was *very* good I was allowed to play with a doll's tea-set which had been Mum's when she was a little girl. It had been given her by the Rector's daughter when Mum was ill. The cups and saucers were extremely small, and rather roughly made, and were kept in a wooden box. Another gift from the same source was a scrap-book. I often wondered where the gaily coloured pictures of children in Victorian costume came from. I have since learned that books of these were sold in Victorian times, and children used to cut out the pictures and stick them in the scrap-books.

As Mum grew older, she acquired a few books from the same kind lady. (The daughter of Rev. Walter Evans.) I remember reading them when I was ill, and desperate for something to read, but even as a child I was repelled by their sentiment. They seemed to be full of children dying most 'improving' deaths. Actually, the infant mortality figures for the period when these books were written reveals that they were not so far-fetched as they seemed to me, but I hardly think they could have cheered Mum any more than they did me. Mum kept them because she had so few books, and she loved reading. In this she was different from the twins, who preferred sewing and knitting.

Sally shared Mum's love of books, but by this time she was no longer at home. Mr. Williams of The Gaer, Forden, who would have been referred to as a gentleman farmer, asked Grandma if one of her daughters would come and keep house for him. He was a bachelor with a young niece, Clara Probert. Sally being the eldest was the one chosen to go. She found herself treated entirely as one of the family, and was expected to act as hostess to the parties of Mr. Williams' friends who came for the shooting and fishing.

At first this terrified her, but she soon learned the expected ways of doing such things as laying the table for these rather elaborate functions, and as there was adequate help in the house she was never overworked. She and Clara became very fond of each other, and Sally remained there happily until Clara returned from boarding school and took over the reins.

Maggie's first experience of housekeeping was very different. Grandma's sister Annie had married Edward Price* and was living at The Vaenor, outside Rhayader. She was rapidly losing her sight, probably from glaucoma. Her husband wrote to ask Grandma if one of her daughters would come and keep house for them, so Maggie went. It was a fairly large farm but they had little or no help in the house. She worked extremely hard, which she didn't mind, for she was very sorry for her Aunt.

But Price was an absolute skin-flint. He begrudged coal for

* *No connection with Grandma Llangurig*

the fire, and the food was like nothing Maggie had experienced. They seemed to live mostly on fat bacon, which she could not digest. Their only son, Teddy, was proud enough when dressed up to go to Rhayader, but for the rest of the time he didn't care how he looked or dressed. Maggie was always slim, but by the time she had been there a year she had shrunk alarmingly.

On one of her visits home Grandma took her to the doctor, who said she must leave The Vaenor immediately. It took over a year to rebuild her strength.

Maggie, Katie and Tom absorbed a good deal of the superstition of the neighbourhood. It was from them that I heard about 'corpse candles' which lighted the way to a house in which someone would shortly die, and a black dog which also haunted the ways of the dead. They didn't actually claim to have seen a ghostly funeral, wending its way along the path which a real one was soon to follow, but they said they knew someone who had. It was only in later years that I realised how old and how widespread these beliefs were in Wales.

Meanwhile Mum attended Castle Caereinion National School (established by the Church of England). It was a long trudge from Pen-y-Byrwydd - and an even longer trudge back up - and there must have been times when snow made the road impassable, but she made good progress in her lessons. She treasured her Scripture Knowledge Certificates, awarded annually after the Diocesan Inspection to which the school was subject in addition to the visits of Her Majesty's Inspectors.

Another treasure Mum kept was a cutting from the **County Times** headed **Empire Day**. :'Owing to being closed for epidemic the school was unable to join the combined demonstration at Welshpool. We regret it very much, but hope for better luck next year. The prizes given by David Davies Esq., M.P., in connection with the League of the Empire, for map-drawing and essay writing, were won by May Jones and Ralph Gittins respectively, and Miss Evans kindly presented them with a few appropriate words. In the afternoon special lessons were given and patriotic songs sung, and all the children wore daisies, rosettes, Empire badges, and their St. George's Club badge. A flag-staff and Union Jack would have been a pleasing addition and would be a great and constant factor to encourage patriotism and loyalty at an early age.'

This was the period of the establishment of Secondary Education in Montgomeryshire, in schools known as County Intermediate Schools. The first and smallest Intermediate school in the county, and one of the smallest in Wales, was at Llanfair Caereinion, which opened in 1894. Mum took her Entrance Examination in 1908. She won a scholarship including free tuition and books. Sally was delighted that Mum would have the chance of the kind of education she herself had wanted, and Grandpa was very proud of her.

The village was almost equi-distant from Welshpool and Llanfair Caereinion, so Mum had a choice of which school she would attend. Welshpool was a thoroughly English area, so much so that Welsh was not even taught as a subject in the school. So because she thought she would have a better chance of learning Welsh she chose Llanfair.

The Welshpool to Llanfair railway which passed near the village had been opened in 1902, and Mum cycled from home to the station, but it was decided that she should stay in lodgings in the town from Monday to Friday, and these she shared with another farmer's daughter. Unfortunately the food provided by their land-lady was dreadful. The climax came when Mum found a sheep's head, complete with eyes, on her plate. From then on the two girls bought their own food.

One day Mum found that when she sliced her loaf the slice fell into four portions. On examining the loaf she could see that someone had cut off a slice and chopped it into four while still on the loaf, with a rather heavy hand. She didn't tell her landlady, but gently asked the maid if she knew anything about it. The young girl collapsed in tears, and admitted she had taken the bread because she was hungry. Mum and Harriet, her co-digger, told the maid to help herself as often as she needed to, but after that she always asked permission first.

Mum loved the school, but there was one disappointment. She was almost the only pupil who didn't already speak Welsh, so that there was no class at the appropriate beginner level for her to join. It was a very small school, and the subjects available were limited. Latin was taught but not French, Botany but not Zoology or Biology. (Shades of Victorian prudery?)

During her first term Mum learned to play hockey and lacrosse, and was chosen for the hockey team. This would involve travelling on Saturdays to play against other schools, and she wasn't sure what Grandma's reaction would be. So the Games Mistress visited Pen-y-Byrwydd to persuade her. Mum remembered Grandma dressed in her black silk dress and black silk apron entertaining her to tea in the front parlour. To Mum's relief permission was granted. She played Centre Forward with great enthusiasm. Unfortunately there are hazards in all sports, and in one match the ball ran up Mum's stick and struck her on the nose. She was left with a small lump on one side of the bridge which caused her some annoyance when she had to wear spectacles in later life because they would never stay straight.

It was a great joy to Mum to have friends who shared her interests and understood her ambitions. Her favourite subjects were Mathematics, Botany and English Literature. Algebra always fascinated her, for she loved problem solving. Botany too became a life-long interest, and she would name the wild flowers on our walks, and could draw them beautifully. But the great gift she passed on to me was her love of Literature. Unfortunately the mistress who taught English Language and Literature and History was a Miss Roberts whose last post had been at the Girls' School at Ruabon. She was always comparing her Llanfair pupils, unflatteringly, with the girls of Ruabon. She also had a sarcastic tongue. It was her habit to read out her pupils' essays to the class, together with highly critical remarks. As a result, Mum's essays grew shorter and shorter.

During the holidays Mum joined in all the activities of the farm, including entertaining visitors. One of these was Mr. Hughes from Welshpool, a member of the family who founded the well-known catering business. He was not very strong and his parents thought a holiday on the farm would do him good. Another occasional visiter was a cousin, Ethel, from Llanidloes, who had a beautiful soprano voice. Whenever she took part in a concert in the Welshpool or Llanfair area she would stay at Pen-y-Byrwydd.

Sometime during her schooldays Mum borrowed the book **Theodosia Ernest**. This is a novel in which the heroine, against the opposition of her parents, becomes a Baptist. The arguments against Believer's Baptism are presented, but she overcomes them point by point. Mum found the book very convincing and told Grandma that she wished to become a Baptist. Grandma asked the curate to try to reconvert her, but to no avail. There was no Baptist Chapel in their neighbourhood, so the matter was allowed to rest for the time being.

Mum took her Junior Central Welsh Board Certificate in 1910, and passed in 7 subjects, with Distinction in Mathematics and Botany. By this time she had decided she wanted to become a school teacher, so she stayed on at school to take the Senior C.W.B. examination.

When she came to the English Literature examination the thought struck her, "Thank Goodness Miss Roberts won't be reading this!" It was as if she had been set free, and she wrote what she really felt, with the result that she had a Distinction in that subject, together with one in Latin, and passes in five other subjects.

Mum returned to school to collect her Certificate, and was picking up her bike from the cycle shed when Miss Roberts joined her. She expressed her pleasure at Mum's result, but admitted to being puzzled at her success in Literature, in view of the *very* short essays she had produced during the course. So, greatly daring, Mum told her of the thought which had come to her during the examination. She added that she felt that it might perhaps help other pupils if Miss Roberts knew the effect she had on some of them.

In those days the only pupils who continued at school after the Senior Certificate were those intending to go to University. Those aiming for Training College to become Certificated Teachers usually began teaching as Probationers until they were 18 years old. It was possible to take an examination prior to going to College which enabled one to spend only one year at College instead of two, and there were classes set up in the County to prepare those taking this course.

Mum would have preferred to have followed the full two-year course at College, and Grand- father, who was immensely proud of her, was quite prepared to let her do so, but on April 25th 1912 he was killed in a ploughing accident.

70

Castle Caereinion. Old Cottages.

Castle Caereinion. The 'old' School (built 1850)
and Parish Church.

Castle Caereinion.
The 'new' School (built 1890)

Llanfair Caereinion County School (on left)
and Railway Station. c. 1905.

Llanfair Caereinion. Old Dolgoch Bridge and the original temporary County Intemediate School. *John Thomas. c. 1894. By permission of the National Library of Wales.*

Shining Llanfair.

JaneKeay 7/94

CHAPTER 8
Learning to Teach - Abermule and Kerry

The family was shattered by Grandpa's sudden death. For a while they continued at Pen-y-Byrwydd, but Mum's plans had to be modified. In December 1912 she began teaching as a probationer at Dolforwyn School, Abermule. This was built on the hillside on the opposite side of the Severn from the village, looking down on the iron bridge which then carried the main road. The bridge has now been by-passed, and a new school was built in the 1950s, but the old building still stands, converted into a very attractive house. There were 4 teachers at this time, including Mum. The Headmaster, Mr. E.B.Williams, was paid £130 per year, his two Uncertificated Assistants £50 each. Mum's salary is not recorded.

As in most schools at that time, there would be more than one class in the same room, and even where they were divided by a partition this was of wood and glass, so that it was easy to see and hear what went on in the next room. In this way a young teacher's work could be supervised, but it was distracting for the pupils, and agonising for a self-conscious teacher.

The classes often covered more than one year-group, usually called a Standard. For instance, Standards 11 & 111 were often placed in one Class, the teacher setting appropriate work for each, and teaching them alternately. The word 'Standard' was used because any child who didn't reach the level expected by the end of the year would be kept down with the younger children until he or she reached the standard required. It was possible to find a backward boy or girl of 14 years of age sitting with 7-year-old children.

Mum took lodgings in the village from Monday to Friday, cycling to and from her home at the weekends. She travelled through Berriew, and at this time two schools were being built there, one by the Church and the other by the Local Authority. Rivalry between them was intense. At home she was expected to help with all the household tasks, so her marking and preparation had to be fitted in during the week. It was a busy life, but she enjoyed it.

71

One morning the villagers woke up to find that all their front gates were missing. Eventually they were found - piled up on the bridge. The pranksters would have had a merry time watching everyone sorting out their own. This was a typical trick for All Fools' Day or Hallowe'en.

In September the headmaster placed her in sole charge of Standard 1V, who would have been 9 to 10 years old. She must have coped because in January 1914, when she was transferred to Kerry Endowed Girls' School she was described as Uncertificated, and no longer as a probationer. She was placed in charge of the Infants.

On the inside wall of the Assembly Hall of Kerry School is a plaque with the following statement:

Kerry Endowed Schools

'These schools were built and furnished by John Naylor Esq. and Mrs. Naylor aided by the following Subscribers:'followed by a list of names. 'Farmers who aided in Carting Materials for the building:' followed by another list.'School Opened Sept. 18th 1868'

This building was a replacement for the original school near the Church. Mr. and Mrs. Naylor lived at Black Hall.

The first recorded school in the village goes back to 1714 and owed its existence to the efforts of the vicar of the time, Rev. John Catlyn. In a letter of 14th May, 1714 he says: 'We intend to build with Brick and to have a little convenient apartment for the M'r (Master) over the school. We intend a sort of Gallery or long chamber where the poor children who will come from far may lodge in bad weather, for the parish is 9 miles long.'

This was a Charity school where it was intended to teach 15 poor children 'at the charity of the parish.'In March 1788, Richard Jones (a purser in the Navy) who was born at Black Hall, left the then enormous sum of £3000 on trust with the vicar, Church-wardens and the owner and occupier of Black Hall, the interest to be used for the purpose of educating, clothing and feeding poor children at Kerry Charity School, and for the subsequent apprenticing of poor boys. This legacy was to be called **The Black Hall Institution** - from which the present school still benefits.

Kerry was founded as a Church School, but after October 1906, when the schools passed under the control of the County Education Committee, staff salaries and equipment were paid for by the County Council. Building expenses became the joint responsibility of the Council and the Church Authorities. The position of the Vicar was still very important, and he was usually the school Correspondent (Clerk to the Managers).

The boys were taught in the Big Hall next to the tower (where the plaque is). There was a fireplace in the middle of one wall, and a classroom opened off the hall for the Infants. The girls occupied the South side of the building (behind the plaque).

Originally the largest classroom had a gallery then used for teaching. Infants would have been seated there in rows on uncomfortable benches. This gallery was removed in December 1908, when more modern desks arrived. A little later the frosted glass windows were replaced by clear glass, and ventilation improved, but heating remained a problem for many years.

One January the Head Mistress recorded three unusually cold days. The thermometer on the Schoolroom wall under the clock was below freezing point at 9 a.m. and reached only 46° F. in the afternoon. It was impossible for children to work in their ordinary places, so they were arranged as near to the fire as possible.

Kerry village is situated among high hills to the South East of Newtown, and the magnificent rolling countryside can be extremely bleak in winter. One February the Headmaster commented that in spite of the terrible wintry gales, some of the worst for a generation, a few boys living over 3 miles from school showed 'rare grit' by battling through and putting in a full week's attendance.

The Kerry Hills have given their name to a famous breed of sheep, and sheep rearing dominated the school calendar and the occupations of the parents. The owners of Black Hall and Brynllywarch, and other gentry had wide estates and raised enormous flocks. Many of the parents were their tenants or employees. Mr.Naylor built a tramway to transport his timber and supplies between his saw-mill on the Brynllywarch estate and Kerry where it met the line to Abermule, and hence to Newtown. This private railway was closed in 1895, but relaid in 1917 to transport prisoners of war to work on this estate, where there was a Prisoner of War Camp. They were engaged in timber felling and making pit and trench props. At least one family still in the area is descended from one of these prisoners.

Families in those days were large, and farming more labour intensive. At the time when Mum taught there the girls numbered 100 and the boys 93. The Headmistress, always referred to as 'The Mistress', was Miss Harding, a native of Kerry, who had been appointed in 1901. She was a Folk Dance enthusiast, and in 1907 we read of 'an Evening Party in the Reading Room (in the village) given to First Class Girls by the Mistress' at which the children 'performed old-fashioned Country Dances and May-pole Dances, the music being supplied by Miss Hughes and elder scholars.'

It is doubtful whether May-pole Dancing was a genuine survival, though Kerry was the kind of place where this might have happened. - The church has a chained Bible, in Welsh, printed in 1690. - But this was the period of the Art and Crafts Movement, and Miss Harding was not alone in her interest in Country Dance. It was the folk-song collector Cecil Sharp who began the revival of interest in Morris Dancing, and by 1909 it was officially recommended to school teachers.

On February 3rd, 1913, the Mistress recorded that afternoon school began and ended half an hour early to enable teachers and some pupils to attend a Morris Dance class in Newtown taught by Miss Morris of the Esperance Guild of Morris Dancers, London. She added that dancing formed part of the Girls' Physical Education.

Unfortunately School was closed from February 6th to 16th by order of Dr. Humphreys owing to an outbreak of Influenza and colds. On their return the girls practised their songs for St. David's Day after play every day for a week, and on March 3rd they celebrated the festival - which had fallen on the previous Saturday - in the presence of the Chairman of the Managers. They had a holiday in the afternoon.

There is no mention of dancing on this occasion, but on April 2nd Mrs. Harrison and Miss Georgina Naylor paid a long visit. Both ladies took an interest in Morris Dances and each gave a 5 shilling book by the Esperance Guild of Morris Dancers for use in the school.

The Reading Room referred to earlier was very important in

the social life of the village. This attractive building, on the opposite side of the road to the school, was erected in 1856 by Mr. John Naylor for the use of the village. Here 'penny readings' were held from 1865, magazines and newspapers including London dailies were provided, and social activities took place on 3 evenings each week. Here too a group of strolling players performed **Maria Marten; or the Murder in the Red Barn.** The Reading Room served as the village social centre until the new Village Hall on the Common Road was opened in 1957.[9]

On April 11th Miss Owen 'severed her connection with the school after 12½ years' work as Infant Teacher'. The girls congratulated her on her approaching marriage and presented her with a silver entré dish subscribed for by all the children. The Mistress gave a set of fish knives and a fish slice.

On April 14th Miss Olive Louisa Williams began work as a supplementary Teacher (Infants) in place of Miss Owen. Miss Harding records that she had come from Newtown Intermediate School, having passed her Junior C.W.B. Examination, and having no previous experience in teaching. What she does not say is that Miss Olive Williams was the daughter of the licensee of the Herbert Arms, and a former pupil of Kerry Girls' School. Olive had won the David Davies Empire Prize for Map Drawing, and a David Davies Scholarship to Newtown Girls' Intermediate School. She was also a good pianist, and very useful as an accompanist to the dancers, having been one of them herself.

On April 29th there was an Annual Holiday for Newtown April Fair. The following day lesons were suspended for the last part of the afternoon to practise Maypole and Morris Dances for May Day.

On May Day itself the children danced Morris Dances on the Village Square, morning playtime being extended to 11.30. This is the first time this event, which became a tradition, is recorded. The Maypole was a portable one, having a 3 or 4-cornered base on which small children sat to keep it firm.

On May 9th school was closed until 13th for Whitsun. Eight girls accompanied by the Mistress went over to Newtown Intermediate School to practise their Morris Dances with the Newtown Class under Miss Mallet in order to assist at Newtown

Garden Fête in aid of the Nursing Association on May 22nd.

On May 19th playtime was extended to enable Mr. Poundley to take photographs of the Maypole and Morris Dance children.[10]

After this the school year proceeded as usual, with the customary high-lights. The Vicar questioned the school in Scripture. The Diocesan Examination took place. There was a holiday for a Rummage Sale in the schools, a half holiday on Empire Day after the Celebration and the presentation of the usual prizes. The Essay set was: 'Which Country would you prefer to emigrate to, Canada or Australia? Give reasons.' The Map to be drawn was Newfoundland. There was a half holiday for the Baptist Sunday School Treat, and a whole day holiday for the Church Sunday School Excursion to Aberystwyth.

The school closed for 5 weeks' Summer holiday on July 25th, attendance for that week being low 'owing to hay-making, fruit picking and whinberry gathering.' In September the school listened to an address on Tuberculosis.

In December Miss Olive Williams began a 13-week course of training as an Infant Teacher at Penygloddfa School, Newtown. It should be borne in mind that she had received no previous training, and that there was no experienced Infant teacher at Kerry to guide her. In January Mum was sent from Dolforwyn to replace Miss Williams for the period of the course. Perhaps it is not surprising that at first Mum gained the impression that she was not entirely welcome to Miss Harding. Olive had been a Prize pupil, and her musical ability far surpassed Mum's. But the Mistress was fundamentally a fair-minded woman, and she soon swallowed her chagrin.

Mum continued to go home for the weekends, cycling down to Abermule to catch the train. It would be a glorious free-wheeling ride most of the way, but the return climb on Monday mornings was a strenuous start to the week.

Soon after her arrival the school was brightened by pictures brought by Mr. Willans of Dolforgan, from the Montgomeryshire Picture Loan Society. The Managers had failed to come up with the subscription to join this scheme, but Mr. Willans generously paid it himself. The three pictures on loan this time were **The Protestant Reformation, The Princes in the Tower,** and a large landscape, **A**

Storm in Harvest.

Mr. Willans, who was a member of the Education Committee, had made other gifts to the school, including wall maps. From time to time he entertained the senior boys and girls at his home, showing them Magic Lantern slides of the British Empire.[11]

There was a national scheme which encouraged children to acquire pen pals in the colonies, but in addition to this, some of the girls were put in touch with pupils from the Happy Valley School near Adelaide, South Australia, described as 'Mrs. Cholmondeley's school - formerly Miss Hilda Naylor of Brynllywarch Hall, Kerry.'

Apart from Reading, Writing and Arithmetic, schools had been expected to teach Needlework, Domestic Economy and Singing, even in the days of 'Payment by Results', when the grant, out of which came the teacher's salary, depended on the report of the Inspector. It is not clear what Domestic Economy entailed, but there was no provision for practical cookery. However, by 1911 Miss Harding was making a great effort to improve matters. On March 2nd she gave what she described as a 'Household Management Lesson': 'Mrs. Willans,* who kindly interests herself in these lessons, gave the girls a fine fore-quarter of mutton to cook for their dinner. The children weighed shoulder, neck and breast. Calculated price at 7 pence per pound, cooked meat. (Roast and Irish Stew). Laid table, boiled potatoes. Invited Teachers to a dinner enjoyed by everybody. Muriel Philips carved parts. A hearty vote of thanks given to Mrs. Willans for her kindness - And to Miss E.Harding for her trouble and use of her kitchen.'

In 1912 a duly qualified teacher was employed by the Education Committee to give the girls a course of Cookery lessons in the Reading Room. They were divided into two groups of 18, and each group received a month's course. In September 1915 16 girls began a course of Domestic Science lessons at the Newtown Centre. The children walked to and from Newtown every Monday.

Needlework for the Senior girls involved garment making, and at Kerry at least the parents were willing to provide their own materials. They began by making a child's pinafore. This would have been a much more elaborate garment than any worn nowadays. It was like a full skirted dress which opened all the way down the back and was fastened by strings at the neck and waist.

*Mother of Mr. J. B. Willans, known as 'Squire Willans'.

Although it was sleeveless it usually had frills on the shoulders, which would stand up prettily above the fashionable 'leg of mutton' sleeves of their dresses. These pinafores, bleached and starched, were worn to school.

First Aid had been taught for quite a few years, and gardening was being introduced, first to the boys, and then the girls were given some of the flower beds to cultivate. Sometimes they had to wait for a promised load of manure. At other times the gate would be left open or the fence broken, and the cattle would get in, destroying their pretty gardens, and then they were dependent on the Vicar and other friends of the school to provide them with seedlings so that they could start again.

Geography and History, in spite of the maps, were still largely confined to the Readers provided by the Education Committee, but gradually the curriculum was widening. Mum, teaching the Infants, developed an interest in the teaching of Reading which remained with her throughout her career.

She made friends too. Just before she was moved to Kerry another young teacher joined the staff. This was a former pupil, Miss Nellie Easthope, a year younger than Mum, who also had passed her Senior Certificate, and was beginning her probationary year. Nellie had an older sister, Hilda, already teaching at the school. Both eventually became fully Certificated Teachers.

They had a brother much younger than themselves, named Colin, who was a pupil in the Infants Class at this time. He and another boy of about the same age, Noel Jerman, had brilliant careers.[12] This speaks well of the standard of teaching at Kerry. Mum was very happy there, and learned much.

On April 8th Miss Olive Williams returned. But meanwhile, on April 3rd, His Majesty's Inspector, Dr. Williams, visited the Boys' School, and was surprised to find they had been without a teacher for the Infants so long. He promised to see to the matter. He also hoped that woodwork would form part of the school curriculum.

On looking back we find that there had been no regular teacher of the Infants since September. As the Head so rightly complained, this had disorganised the work of the whole school. He was very pleased when Mum turned up after the Easter holiday.

On May 1st he recorded that the school had been closed on

78

the previous Tuesday for the Annual April Pleasure Fair at Newtown, but there is no mention of May Day in the Boys' School log book. Empire Day figures, with a special programme of Songs, Recitations and Addresses substituted for the ordinary timetable, and a holiday in the afternoon. This was an important occasion all over the country, and in Montgomeryshire the M.P., David Davies, had established the prizes awarded. He was a Liberal and a Non-conformist, and therefore unlikely to appeal to everyone, especially to Conservatives and Churchmen, but it is undeniable that he did a great deal for education in this county. The scholarships, however, had been given in memory of the first David Davies by his son Edward and his widow in 1891, and provided the winners with either a bicycle or the cost of transport, and with books, at the beginning of their secondary schooling.

During the Summer Term the children usually went on a walk to collect Cowslips or primroses which they sent to Dr. Barnardo's Hospital for Crippled Children. There was also an annual outing for the senior pupils, often to Laburnum Wood, or to Cwmydalfa, and the site of Pen Castle (Hubert's Folly). They were encouraged to take an interest in Nature Study, and made collections of wild flowers, for which prizes were given at the Village Show.

Mr. Noel Jerman recalled playing football in the playground, and on the street by the New Inn (now the Kerry Lamb). Other games were conkers (when the chestnuts were ripe) tip-it and marbles, though the latter had to wait until the March winds had dried out the road, there being no tar-macadam then.

On September 1st comes the first reference to the outbreak of the Great War. The Headmaster writes:'There is only a fair attendance. Owing to a scarcity of labour as a result of the European War, many children are being kept at home to work in the harvest fields.'

Not that this was the only cause, for on September 4th he commented that the sheep auction held near the station had greatly interfered with attendance. This was in addition to the Annual Sheep Fair held in the village on the 16th, for which the schools were closed as usual. A previous headmaster made out the case that it was an important part of the boys' education, as well as a help to their fathers, that they should attend. He even recorded the highest price bid for a ram. Meanwhile the Headmistress complained that it was impossible to open school because they wouldn't have been able to get near the gate.

The whole of the centre of the village was filled with sheep pens, the hurdles being easily driven between the cobbles of the pavements. The householders were each paid by the individual farmers for the use of the pens outside their houses.

The closures for the Fairs at Newtown in March, April, May, September and October, in addition to Harvest Thanksgivings and Annual Treats for both Church and Chapel, didn't in fact reduce the number of days the school had to be open. Those were fixed by law. If the schools were closed often for illness as well there was a danger that the time would have to be made up by shortening the holidays, and on one occasion a school had to open on a Saturday to avoid this.

There were no major epidemics during Mum's time at Kerry, but the seriousness of such occurrences is borne out by a recent statement in the Press: 'Between 1850 and 1950 the death rate from tuberculosis, diptheria, scarlet fever, enteric fever, whooping cough and measles was cut by 99 per cent - in part by immunisation programmes and new drugs, but more importantly through such non-medical measures as clean water, safe sewage, better housing and improved working conditions.'

No doubt the visits of the School Doctor, Nurse and Dentist played an important part in the gradual improvement.

In October Mr. Willans visited the school, bringing with him two Belgian refugees. One of these, aged 12 years, became a pupil at the school.

On December 18th when the Kerry schools closed for the Christmas holidays, Mum left to take up an appointment at Castle Caereinion, and was replaced by Miss Easthope.

Kerry School (left), Reading Room (right), and Church (in background)

Kerry Village from Collection of J. D. K. Lloyd. Many of the trees in the picture were felled during World War I. *By permission of the National Library of Wales.*

The Chained Bible in Kerry Church.
Photo taken by the late Noel Jerman, CBE, MA, FSA.
In J. D. K. Lloyd Collection.
By permission of the National Library of Wales.

Abermule Station : The Kerry Branch Line.
In J. D. K. Lloyd Collection.
By permission of the National Library of Wales.

My mother, Mary Jane Jones (known as May).

My mother's twin sisters, Maggie and Katie.

Chapter 9
Teaching at Castle Caereinion and Llandinam

The schools in the county didn't all begin their holidays on the same date, probably because some had to make up for occasional closures. Although Kerry schools had broken up for the Christmas holidays, Castle Caereinion was still open, and on December 21st Mum took up her duties there, under Mr. James Smith. They closed on December 23rd, and re-opened on January 18th with a new Head-master, Mr. R.E.Morris. On the same day a new Supplementary Teacher, Miss S.A.James, was appointed. This indicates that the previous staff had arranged that their resignations should all take effect at the same time - not a good sign.

In later years Mum warned me that it is not an easy matter to return as a teacher to the school where you were a pupil. She went home in order to help her mother, but she found she was still regarded as a young girl, and had to struggle to obtain the respect necessary to hold her position in the school and community. Also Maggie had left home, and Katie who was often ill relied on Mum to help with many of the household tasks.

Another factor was the new Rector, Rev. W. Gwynne Vaughan. When he succeeded Rev. Evans he had told his parishioners, "I have come to live with you and to die with you," which caused some consternation. It was, however, truly his privilege as Rector to hold the living as long as he chose. The school of 76 boys and girls was a Church foundation, and the Rector was not only Correspondent but also Chairman of the Managers. He often took Scripture lessons with the top class, and visited the school frequently at other times.

At first all went well. Mum and Miss James were allowed to leave school at 2.30 p.m. on Fridays in order to attend a teachers' Class at Newtown. This continued on Saturday mornings. It was led by Mr. Lane Griffiths, the Headmaster of Penygloddfa School, Newtown, one of the best qualified and most effective teachers in the county. This was the two-year course intended to prepare teachers for an examination which would shorten the time required

81

for the Certificate Course to one year in College instead of two. It meant a great deal of extra work, but Mum was eager to qualify.

In April it was decided that new lamps were badly needed and these were paid for by the funds raised at a Children's Concert. In May a circular arrived from the Y.M.C.A. appealing for money to construct huts for the soldiers, which were to be called 'Children's Huts'. A collection was made, and 9 shillings and 4 pence was forwarded to the Secretary.

1916 began with two months of exceptionally bad weather, culminating in a snow fall at the end of February which prevented both Assistants from reaching school, and reduced attendance to 23 children.

By April Miss James had left, and the headmaster was understandably annoyed to find her replacement, Miss Bowen, appointed without even informing him. There was clearly friction between him and the Rector.

On June 7th Mr. Morris recorded that 'The school flag was hoisted at half-mast today in token of the grave loss the nation had sustained through the death of Lord Kitchener, the Secretary of State for War.'

The school closed on July 14th, to re-open on August 28th. The closure was earlier than usual, 'owing to the present shortage of labour on account of the war.' But after the new term began the attendance was 'below average owing to harvest operations.' This entry, for September 7th, is the last from Mr. Morris. The Rector states on September 8th that 'the school this day is in charge of Miss Jones and Miss Bowen. Miss Davies, the new Headmistress, commences duty on Monday next, the 11th.'

It may seem strange that Mr. Morris should give notice to expire at the beginning of a term, but had he left at the end of the previous term he would have had no pay for the holidays. This applied to the long Summer holiday.

In October 1916 Mum was taken seriously ill. The cause was diagnosed as anaemia. She became very weak and depressed, and remained at home for 4 months. When the wind was in one direction she could hear the school bell, and morning and afternoon she heard the chatter of the children as they passed the house on their way to and from school. At times she couldn't hold back her tears at the thought that she might never be able to return to teaching, but at last, at the end of February 1917 she was back at school. She decided, however, to give up the Teachers' Course, and to remain an Uncertificated teacher.

Changes had been taking place in the family. Sometime before this Tom had emigrated to America, but he was less fortunate than Dad's brother Gwilym in that he had no relatives to help him in the early stages, and after about a year he returned. While there he picked up a few Negro Spirituals and songs like **Carry Me Back to Old Virginie**, which he used to sing to his own accompaniment on the violin. He was self-taught, practising in the stable of whatever farm he was working on, having been chased out of the house. He had a pleasant tenor voice, and in later years was a member of the choir of local talent gathered together by the Misses Davies of Gregynog to take part in their famous musical evenings.

Tom also liked to paint landscapes and to write light topical verse. It is a pity he didn't continue with his education long enough to develop some of these gifts. He always seemed more interested in them than in farming. Another of his talents was the ability to charm warts. He never divulged the method, perhaps believing that to do so was to risk losing the power.

After Tom's return, in May 1916 Joel, the eldest son, got married, and he and his wife Harriet moved to Hiriad, which they eventually bought. In the following April Tom married Sis (short for Cecily) and moved to Glan Edyr, near New Mills. Life became more difficult for Grandma. She tried to continue at Pen-y-Byrwydd by employing more men, but these were hard to come by in wartime, and the farm became less profitable.

At school 1918 began unpromisingly. - The floor had not been washed during the holidays, and there was an epidemic of Whooping Cough which closed the school for a month. On their return they found that the caretaker had left. The fires were not lit, so the children were sent out to play, in order to keep warm until the fires were lit by the teachers. Thereafter, Miss Davies and Mum arrived at school at 8.10 a.m. to try to get the rooms warm enough to begin school at the proper time, but the place became more and more dirty. It wasn't until March 11th that a new caretaker started work.

These were probably not the only problems. Once more there was friction between the Rector and the Head Teacher. Mum thought highly of Miss Davies, and was grieved to see yet another able teacher frustrated. The real trouble was that Rev. Gwynne Vaughan, who was genuinely interested in the school, couldn't get used to the changes which had taken place in education. He hankered after the old system in which the Rector reigned supreme. Still less could he accept a position in which a *woman* might stand up to him and claim the right to organise her own school. Miss Davies was a strong personality, deeply committed to teaching, and she eventually decided it was better to move to a school where she could see her ideas carried out without continual criticism.

She discussed this with Mum, who realised that she would herself be in a difficult position if she remained after Miss Davies left, since she had made no secret of her support for the Headmistress. Katie was rather shocked that Mum should criticise the Rector, but Grandma understood. She may not have agreed, but she didn't want Mum to continue working in an atmosphere of strife. So Mum went to see the Clerk to the Education Committee, Mr. Llewelyn Phillips, who later became the first Director of Education for Montgomeryshire. There was a vacancy at Llandinam, so Mum gave in her notice, which expired on March 21st. Miss Davies also left at the end of that term.

Llandinam

Llandinam School, where Mum began work on April 17th, in charge of Standards 11 & 111, had been closed for the previous month - 3 weeks owing to an outbreak of Scabies, and 1 week for the Easter holiday.

For the first time Mum found herself in a Council (formerly a Board) School. The influence of Church and Chapel in the village had been more or less equal when the school was founded, and both were represented on the Managers. The chief families at that time were the Crewe-Reads of Plas Dinam and David Davies then at Broneirion. Both supported the foundation and paid the fees for their tenants' children. By 1918, when Mum taught there, the Crewe-Reads had left the village, and David Davies, grandson of the Coal Owner and Railway Builder, was living at Plas Dinam, and representing Montgomeryshire in Parliament. After he resigned his seat in 1929 he became the first Lord Davies.

The peace between the religious denominations went back quite a long way in Llandinam, for B.Bennet Rowlands, writing of the old church which was almost rebuilt in 1865, says:[13] 'It was the custom in my younger days for the Nonconformists to attend the Church Services at say about 12 noon when their own services would be over. They came into the Gallery and therefore would not distract the congregation, they and the Church-going people fraternizing and helping each other in all religious activities.'

The village was very attractive, although the white bungalows which front the main road had yet to be built. The old black and white and the grey stone cottages, and Llandinam Hall, stood as they had for many years. Newer buildings included the red brick Village Hall, and the Chapels. The Parish Church had been renovated not long before, and the village bake-house provided by Captain Crewe Read in 1870 was still in use, as was the Lion (formerly The Mermaid), the Forge, the Railway station, and the iron bridge with the statue of the original David Davies studying his map (a duplicate of the one at Barry Docks which he built.) The Lion, however, was a 'Temperance Hotel', for Llandinam, under the influence of David Davies, was a 'dry' village. Much of it belonged to him, and he had rebuilt many of the houses.

Mum didn't stay in the village itself, but in Pwllan Cottages, about 1 mile away. As she cycled to and fro she passed another teacher on her way to Llanidloes - a lady who was to become Mrs. Garbett Edwards. Mum no longer went home every weekend, so she took part in Church activities such as the Girls' Friendly Society which she had joined in 1910 in Castle Caereinion.

Soon she grew friendly with the Vicar and his wife, Rev. and Mrs. James Jones. She became a Sunday School teacher, and helped with the Sunday Teas held at the Vicarage. Because many parishioners lived a long way from the village, Mrs. Jones provided a meal so that they didn't have to make the journey twice. Those who had attended Morning Service were welcome to lunch as well.

It being war time, provisions were scarce, so Mrs. Jones mixed potatoes with flour to produce scones which were very filling. It was the rule that scones had to be eaten before any of the other goodies were enjoyed.

The curate became interested in Mum, and she went out with him a few times, but she didn't take him very seriously. During her discussions with Rev. Jones she revealed her interest in Believers' Baptism, and he said he would be perfectly willing to baptise her. However, she felt she wanted to be baptised by someone who believed in it as she did.

At school the Head had formed a Scholarship class of 11 pupils, and invited Mum to assist, since the extra teaching was given mainly after school hours. All of these sat the Scholarship Examination, 7 at Llanidloes and 4 at Newtown. 7 obtained entrance, 4 of them with scholarships.

The children worked hard for the War effort too. The woodwork class had been making splints for wounded soldiers, and on one occasion 12 Angular Arm Splints, 25 Straight Arm Splints, 78 finger splints together with one netted Hammock were sent to the St. Marylebone War Hospital Supply Depot, London.

The girls had not been idle either. The Christmas Parcel from the school contained 50 pairs of mitts, 2 scarves, 30 handbags and 10 pairs of cuffs.

On July 8th The Head attended the Army Medical Board. On July 12th he complained of a low attendance for the previous fortnight owing to whinberry picking and the hay harvest. Many children sold whinberries and bought eggs with the proceeds. Others collected eggs from home and from their neighbours. These eggs were frequently sold or sent to Hospitals in aid of wounded soldiers.

This was the only Primary School where Mum taught in which there was any attempt to teach Welsh, and here it seemed to be solely due to the Head, who decided to teach the upper classes.

October brought an epidemic of Influenza which closed the school. Mum had a severe attack and was visited several times by the doctor. She was rather worried that she must be running up a large bill, but he consoled her with the words, "I have to visit Plas Dinam anyway. Mrs. Davies will be paying the bill."

She was able to return to school when it re-opened after 3 weeks, and continued teaching there until the Christmas Holidays, when she was appointed to take charge of Pantmawr School, above Llangurig. She had asked to move because she had developed a goitre. The doctor told her they were prevalent in the village, and he thought it might be the result of something in the soil, or the low-lying situation of the village, and advised Mum to tell Mr. Llewelyn Phillips, Clerk to the Education Committee, which she did.

His reply was, "Well, if the valley doesn't suit you we'll see what the hills will do."

Pantmawr was the highest school in the County.

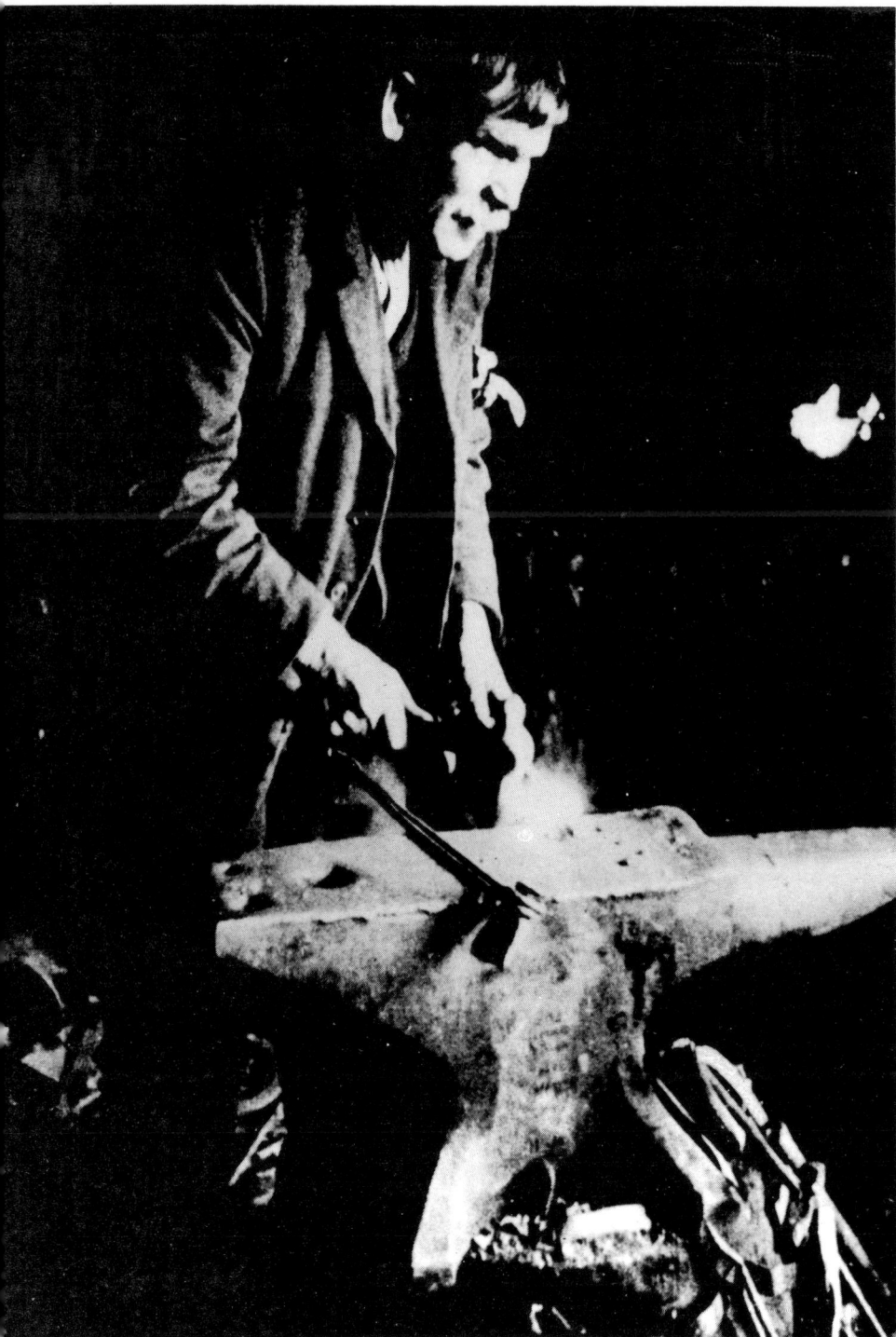

The late Mr. John Pryce at the Old Forge, Llandinam.

Llandinam Smithy c. 1910. Mr. J. Pryce (on horseback) and family.

The Old Bakehouse, Llandinam, demolished in the 1960s.

Llandinam : Plas Dinam c. 1904

Llandinam : View from Church Walk.

Llandinam Post Office

Llandinam Village c. 1904

Chapter 10
Courtship: Pantmawr and Ellerdine

Pantmawr School was established at the Western end of Llangurig Parish to cater for the children who lived too far away to attend the Council School in the village. It was built at the side of the main road to Aberystwyth, just beyond Capel Uchaf, the 'Upper Chapel' of the Methodists whose Capel Isaf was at Dernol. Below the chapel is the cottage called Ty'n Llechwedd, which is still Pantmawr Post Office The school building is now a hotel and restaurant. There are two cottages alongside the school, A mile past the school comes the Glan-Severn Arms Hotel, and a little further still towards Aberystwyth comes Siop Newydd cottage, whose owner used to keep a little shop, and that is all. Beyond stretches the Plynlimon (or Pumlumon) mountain range.

Looking at it today one might wonder not that the school has closed, but that it was ever opened. Its most distinguished former pupil, Dr. E.Arthur Lewis, Professor of Welsh History at U.C.W. Aberystwyth, explains in his recollections of the school[14]:

'Pantmawr was originally a school for the children of the miners and the children of the shepherds.' - There were lead mines at Nanty, (He was born at Nanty Farm.) Nantiago, Nant yr Eira and Siglen Las. When he attended, from about 1892, there were approximately 50 pupils, more than enough for some merry and some riotous games.

Because of the slant of the yard it was not suitable for marbles, so they had to draw the ring on the turnpike road - safe enough in those days. Another game which was played across the road was pitching quoits. There was a plentiful supply of stones for this purpose, thanks to the old Highways Board. Occasionally horseshoes were obtained, but once during such a game there was a nasty accident, and one of the boys had a scar under his left eye from that day on. They also played at wrestling, hop, skip and jump, and racing. There was little room for football as such. The annual big football match of the district was a game with the Old Boys by moonlight on Hendre. (Dr. Lewis later played for Wales). Few children lived near enough to go home for dinner. Some went to neighbouring families. Dr. Lewis sympathetically describes most of them as 'children of the slice of buttered bread and the bottle of milk.' They went fishing in the lunch hour, in Nant Tynycwm for pilks, preparing for the time when they would fish the Wye and the Bidno - often by night. In the winter term they went skating on Hendre pool. In Spring they searched for birds' nests and crows' and magpies' eggs in Tynllechwedd and Llwynhyddod woods, also in their season for nuts, blackberries, raspberries and flowers.

If they were late returning after lunch they knew what to expect, for 'Old Keighley', the first English headmaster - an eccentric with white waistcoat and gold watch-chain - was a disciplinarian of the old style. If the cane failed to restore order he would try a big brush, and if that was ineffectual he would threaten them with the chopper - and peace would reign in the little group which a few minutes before he had described as 'boiling mad.'

He was a conscientious and careful teacher except in Music, but fortunately a local lady conductor came to coach them in one or two songs for the examination.

Keighley's favourite hymn was 'Work for the night is coming.' Once he fell into a whirlpool in the River Wye, but was rescued. He wept like a child when speaking of his narrow escape. For years after retiring to Yorkshire he sent bundles of old newspapers for the pleasure and enlightenment of his old pupils still living in that 'outlandish place.'

Dr. Lewis recalled the old curriculum, taught in late Victorian style, the slates and slate-rags only slowly replaced by exercise books and pencils. While the school was a Board School (i.e. before it became a 'Council School') the curriculum was on the lines of the 1870 code, with not much of a Welsh flavour, but fortunately some Welsh elements came from Chapel and home - stories, songs and ballads. The aim of the teaching was to master a few things, with the 3Rs (Reading, Writing and Arithmetic) as the nucleus. This was broadened under two very able headmistresses who followed Keighley.

The climax of the school year was the Examination Day. The

little school was as clean as a new pin, everyone clothed in Sunday best. As a rule the Inspector came in the afternoon. This was rather a disadvantage to the scholars who had come splendidly dressed in the morning.

'The Chief Inspector (Rev. Temple) came to Pantmawr, without exception, just as he always delegated to his Assistant, Mr. Johnson, less important schools.'

An old boy of the school would call to inform them that he had passed the Inspector making his leisurely way past Pencrugyn - about two miles away - at about 1.30. This was the signal for the final rehearsal of the pupils'

"Good Afternoon, Sir."

Then the appointed scout stationed at the milestone stating "Llanidloes 8 miles" would burst in with the news, "He's coming now." At last, after a long wait, here came Inspector Temple in all his dignity.

Mr. Temple examined and was very happy with the Registers, and the Log-book, and the samplers of the girls. After working at sums and reading, they sang a song or two, such as **Men of Harlech**, and recited, each in turn, a few lines of **John Gilpin**, **The Pet Lamb** or **Lucy Grey**. And that was the end of the examination for another year.

The outstanding social day of the year was the day of the Clochfaen Tea Party. This was established soon after the arrival of Chevalier Lloyd's heiress and her husband Colonel Verney to live at Clochfaen. The Verneys were a great acquisition for the life of Llangurig village and district in many ways. But none was more important in the eyes of the community than the Annual Treat for the school children of the district, held on the birthday of their daughter Morforwyn Lloyd Verney, August 6th.

The first occasion was unforgettable. - Besides Tea, Toys, Sports, Fireworks, Prizes for Good Conduct, Industry, Needlework etc., etc., each child received 'a new shilling with the Lion mark' and a Post Office Savings Bank Book. The Annual Treat was maintained, and it was a splendid sight on a sunny August afternoon to see the scholars of the three * schools marching two abreast across Bont y Llan. On this occasion the children of Llangurig and Pantmawr were rather jealous of the children of

90

* Dernol was not opened until 1907.

Cwmbelan -

'We had walked in order the whole way, but the Cwmbelan children were *driven* to Llangurig village - and in pomp at that - in a big *decorated* wagon by that genial man Lloyd bach of Glyngynwydd.'

When Mum arrived at Pantmawr there was still no school house, so she had to take lodgings in Llangurig, 3 miles away, with Mrs. Jones, Rock Villa (now Bryn Awel). Her fellow lodger was the District Nurse, Nurse Pritchard. (Later to become Mrs. Nicholas, and the Matron of Caersws Workhouse)

On January 7th 1919 Mum proudly recorded:

'I re-opened school this morning after the Christmas holidays. There were 13 children present. (Number on books - 14) I have been appointed Head Mistress of this school.'

Within a week the numbers were increased when Howell John Evans and Richard Emrys Evans of Llwynhyddod were re-admitted. They had been attending Llangurig School, but their parents thought the distance too great. Sadly, during that first week she also had to record the death of one of the pupils, a little girl, and the attendance at the funeral of her cousins.

As might be expected for a school among the foothills of Plynlimon, the weather had a crucial effect on teacher and pupils alike. At the end of January there was a severe snowstorm, which continued into February, attendance gradually falling, until only two turned up, and the school was officially closed for a week. Mum often became soaked on her way to school, but on many occasions one of the Evans boys from Plas-y-Bwlch would cycle home to fetch a dress belonging to his sister Myfanwy, who was about the same size as Mum, so that she could change, and dry her own clothes in time to go home. Around the stove she would also hang the children's socks and their coats. Like them she brought her own sandwiches for lunch, and she boiled a kettle for mugs of cocoa for them all.

She met with other kindnesses too. On very cold mornings an old lady who lived in a cottage she passed used to stand at her doorway with a cup of tea, and a hot potato, which Mum clutched in her pocket, warming her hands in turn as she pushed her bike up the long hills.

Not everyone was so sympathetic. One farmer decided to keep a close watch on the new teacher, and positioned one of his sons, either hedging or ditching, in a roadside field at the time when she was due to pass in the morning. This so annoyed her that when she met the man in the village she told him she was sorry for his sons, getting cold in the mornings. "Don't bother to set them to time me," she said. "I'll ring my bell so you'll be sure to hear me from your house." And so she did, loud and long, every morning.

In spite of the closure during February, the pupils presented suitable items on St. David's Day before their visitors, Rev. Edward Evans and his daughters. Rev. Evans, who was the Methodist Minister, gave them an appropriate address. He was the School Correspondent, and seems to have played a similar rôle to the Vicar in a Church school. March brought further snow falls, reducing attendance to one child on several days, and at the end of the month an influenza epidemic closed the school for a week. But as Spring brought better weather the attendance and the number on the Register increased.

Mum's landlady, Mrs. Jones, was a match-maker, and set about finding a suitable young man for Mum. At the week-ends she entertained any visiting preacher engaged by the Methodist chapel, and during the following week the Treasurer called to pay her for this service. Often he would be there when Mum returned from school, and on one occasion she heard them discussing her.

Mrs. Jones had decided that one of her favourite preachers would be an excellent choice for Mum, but the old deacon strongly disagreed. "I'll find a young man for Miss Jones," he declared. "You leave it to me."

Mum was quite grateful that he had intervened in what was becoming a rather embarrassing situation. She was all the more taken aback when some time later he announced, "I've found the very man for Miss Jones. Orlie the Tailor has come back home. He's just the one for her."

This announcement was enough to keep Mum well away from the Tailor's shop where she had been used to chatting to Grandma while choosing patterns etc.

Summer came, bringing more children to school. Eventually the roll grew to 19. Had it reached 20 another teacher might have been appointed, but the lead mines were becoming less profitable, and closing down. The miners no longer lived with their families in cottages near the mines. Instead they walked home at the weekends - most of them lived at Ysbytty Ystwyth - and a lády went up from Llangurig to clean their cottages. It was a long trek home, across the Plynlimon foothills, and to guide them on dark and foggy nights they placed white quartz stones along the sides of the road or track. It was an ancient way, used in former times by drovers taking the Cardiganshire cattle to markets in the Midlands and further afield.

Some of the children walked two and three miles to school. Conditions had not improved much since Dr. Lewis' time. The stove was smokey, and there was no supply of drinking water. It had to be fetched in a bucket from a well at the side of the road, 50 yards away. Mrs. M.J.Morgan* who was a pupil at this time relates how she used to bring a bottle of milk to school, and in summertime would refill it with spring water on the way home. When she was hungry she would sometimes 'pinch' turnips. They played Fox and Hounds up the side of the hill behind the school, and Rounders on the school yard.

There was the usual half-holiday for Empire Day, breaks for Singing Festivals, both Church and Chapel, held in Llanidloes, and a holiday for Whit Monday. During one of these breaks Mum and Nurse decided to take their crochet work with them and walk along the old road which went up past the Blue Bell Inn, the School, the shop and the Wesleyan Chapel, and out onto .the moors between Llangurig and Llanidloes. Mum was very fond of crochet and hairpin work, and they thought the weather fine enough to sit out in the sun and continue working. But they needed to buy some more crochet cotton, so they stopped at the shop. There Grandma asked where they were going, and then called Dad, and introduced him. Grandpa had asked Dad to deliver a suit to Nantgwyn Farm, and he seized the opportunity and invited the two young ladies to accompany him.

Nurse already knew Dad, and seemed keen on the suggestion, so Mum fell in with the change of plan. But Dad intended calling at Bwlch y Garreg, a farm on the way to Cwmbelan, to collect his friend Jack Davies, Mary's brother-in-law, who would

93

* I am indebted to Mrs. Morgan for allowing me to use her copy - perhaps the last - of Professor E. Arthur Lewis' book.

be sure to know the way from there to Nantgwyn. This lay along a track across the hills. Dad went in to ask Jack to accompany them, while Nurse and Mum waited outside. Jack was eager to come, but he said to Dad,

"You'll never let me have my choice of which of them I walk with."

Rather reluctantly Dad agreed, and was amazed when Jack chose Nurse, because "She's a good mover," exactly (as Dad thought) 'as if she had been a pony.'

So Dad had his wish and walked with Mum. Nurse and Jack went on ahead, and Nurse seemed quite happy with the arrangement. Mum, however, felt she was being taken for granted, and when Dad offered to take her arm to help her along a rough patch of the road she refused, saying she could manage.

It was quite a long walk, and when they arrived they were invited into the house. Dad entered first and delivered his parcel, and then introduced Nurse Pritchard and Mum as the District Nurse and Miss Jones, the new teacher at Pantmawr. The family were Prices, relatives of his mother. They were all made welcome and pressed to stay to tea. Dad was brought to the fireside to give his aunt and uncle all the news of the family, while Mum sat as far away as possible, on an upright chair near the door.

Mrs. Price was seated on the settle in the shadow, dressed in a black gown with a white lace-edged collar and cap, like someone from a previous century. All the time that Dad was talking she kept gazing at Mum.

Eventually she asked outright, "Who would your people be, my dear?"

To Dad's surprise, Mum said her mother was one of the Lewises of Pen y pistyll, St. Harmons, less than four miles from Nantgwyn.

Mrs. Price immediately stood up and said, "You must be Maggie's daughter. She was my best friend." And she crossed the room with her arms spread wide, and hugged her.

Soon tea was ready and the guests were summoned to the table. Dad and Mum were placed side by side, though neither of them could understand how this had been worked out, and all through the meal Uncle kept referring to the time 'When you two are married.' He wouldn't listen to a word of their explanation that this was the first time they had been out together. Dad was really very amused about this but Mum was extremely embarrassed.

Eventually tea was over and their goodbyes were said. While they had been at Nantgwyn there had been a shower, and on the way back they came to a part where the road sloped and was slippery. Mum would have been pleased to have taken Dad's arm, but it wasn't offered.

When Jack next met Dad he enquired how he had got on with Miss Jones, and Dad replied "Oh, she's a great deal too independent for me."

Despite Mum's reserve their friendship developed, and Dad, who had often been around the village in the early hours of the morning formed the habit of pumping up the tyres of Mum's bike before she set off for school. There seemed no improvement in his insomnia, and one morning he looked more depressed than usual. When Mum asked the reason he said he had been sitting on the seat in the middle of the village when he passed out. When he came to himself he didn't know how long he had been unconscious.

"You weren't unconscious. You fell asleep," she said.

"That's strange," said Dad. "That's what my mother said."

Neither of them really believed their explanation, but they managed to convince him, and the next night he had the first night's sleep for many months.

Gradually he began to recover his health, and wondered what to do about earning a living. His doctor, in view of the possibility of tuberculosis, thought it unwise for him to take up any occupation which would keep him in-doors much of the time, but he wasn't yet robust enough for manual work. Eventually Grandpa suggested that Dad should go around the markets taking orders for breeches and suits. He introduced Dad to the firms with whom he himself had dealt for years, and taught him how to measure a customer.

Mum loved her work at Pantmawr. In so small a school she naturally came to know all the pupils very well. But it wasn't, and still isn't, an easy task being the only teacher to a group of children aged from 5 to 14 years. Keeping all the pupils occupied with work appropriate to each one's age and ability requires skill and fore-thought. Resources are not as freely available as in a larger school,

95

and all problems have but one solution - ask Teacher. Nevertheless, the closure of such schools impoverishes the communities to which they belong. Now-a-days it is Llangurig School which watches its intake anxiously, hoping to preserve the last school in the Parish.

In Mum's day there were 4 schools. On September 15th she wrote:

'A half-holiday was given on Friday. The scholars of this school joined those of the other 3 schools in the village. They marched up to Clochfaen where their treat, given by Lady Joan Verney, was held.'

(The other schools would have been Llangurig Council School, Dernol School and Cwmbelan.)

There would have been Games and races, an excellent tea, and small presents to take home. One year the girls were given small work-baskets.

The School Treat had been suspended during the War, but was re-established afterwards on a new date. On October 3rd Lady Joan and Miss Joy Verney visited the school to award prizes for Needlework and for Progress. [15]

Mum's appointment as Head Teacher was only temporary. The Education Committee had met in April and informed the Managers of the Llangurig Group of Schools that they intended appointing a Certificated Teacher when Miss Jones had completed 6 months at Pantmawr. The post was advertised and the Managers examined the applications, recommending a lady who was fluent in Welsh. Mum had apparently admitted that she found her lack of Welsh a disadvantage - and since 1910 it had been official policy that children should be taught to read and write in their first language.

The appointment was not made until October, and the successful applicant, Miss M.E.Morris, (not the lady the Managers had recommended) took up her duties in November.

Mum had begun to accompany Dad to Concerts, Eisteddfodau and Festivals in the district. Meanwhile he was gradually building up his reputation as a tailor and trader in men's clothing. He never actually made clothing, but took measurements, helped the customer to select the cloth, and sent off the order to manufacturers, with whom the small-scale local tailor could no longer compete. He rented stalls in the Market Halls in Llanidloes, Newtown, Montgomery, Welshpool and Oswestry, and attended Rhayader market on Fair days.

He travelled by train, packing his goods in a wicker skip which he pushed along on a set of wheels which he could carry into his compartment after putting the skip into the guard's van. By this time his youngest brother, Victor, had married and he and his wife Lil were living in Hafren Terrace, Llanidloes. Sometimes Dad stayed with them overnight, which made it much easier to travel. In some of the Market Halls he could board up the stall with shutters when the market closed, so that it formed a little room.

On the night of the 1919 October Fair in Llanidloes Mum came to meet him after the Market closed. Maybe he had intended a walk in the moonlight, but it was pouring with rain, so they took shelter in Dad's stall. It was there that he proposed, and was accepted.

Ellerdine

In December 1919 Mum took up a post in Ellerdine, Shropshire. She found she was paid more as an Assistant in Shropshire than as a Head Teacher in Montgomeryshire.

There could be no greater contrast than that between mountainous Pantmawr and the flat Shropshire plain of which Ellerdine Heath forms a part. The village lies north of Wellington, a market town now almost swallowed up by Telford. The nearest station was at Crudgington, from where Mum would cycle. When she was appointed she thought cycling would be much easier in Shropshire, but if there was no need to push the bike up hill, neither could she free-wheel down. She had to keep on pedalling all the way.

She lodged with Mr. and Mrs. Buttery at their farm, Heath Lanes, Cold Hatton. Mr. Buttery was a River Bailiff, and Mrs. Buttery had been a cook. They had an orchard which produced good cooking and dessert apples and plums, an excellent vegetable garden and they raised poultry. Mum was never better fed than

97

while staying there, and it was from Mrs. Buttery that she had her first taste of eels. These Mr. Buttery had caught, and they were considered a great delicacy. Mum described them as too earthy for her taste.

The headmaster was Mr. Bray, a strict disciplinarian, but a kindly man beneath his martinet's appearance. He showed Mum great understanding, and her friendship with his family was a lasting one. Mum taught the class below Mr. Bray's and assisted with the Scholarship preparation. In this school the Music lessons in all the classes would be in Old Notation one week and Tonic Sol-fa the next.

Mum taught Needlework to the girls while Mr. Bray taught the boys Woodwork.

Previously the girls had not made garments, but only small articles. Some of their parents were not willing to buy material for garments on the grounds that it might be spoiled. So Mum bought enough for the senior girls, and when they had completed their embroidered nightdresses she put them on display, and invited the parents to buy them. There was never any problem after that.

Like most teachers of the time, Mr. Bray used the cane, but Mum never did. She said that no-one of her size could hope to rule by fear.

One wet lunch hour, Mr. Bray having gone home, she was eating her sandwiches in her own room while keeping an eye on the children in the big room who were sheltering from the rain. Suddenly she heard a crash, and some of the smaller children came running in to tell her that William, one of the big boys, had broken a chair.

William was a rather backward pupil who sometimes worked off his frustration by bullying the little ones. When Mum went into the room she saw him running out into the yard. In the middle of the room was the chair - which Mum knew to have come apart previously.

She sent for the culprit, and shut the other children in her own room. Then, without telling William that the chair had collapsed before, she told him to put the glue-pot on the stove, and helped him stick the chair together. When they had finished and parked the chair in a safe place, she told him she was going to forbid the other children to tell Mr. Bray what had happened, on condition that he promised not to be so rough with pupils or furniture in future. At this he put his head down and sobbed. He said he had expected a thrashing. From that day on he was her champion - and no child dared to cause her trouble!

Mrs. Buttery was fond of whist drives and dancing, and Mum went with her when these were held locally. Soon she had friends of her own age with whom she would cycle to social events in the surrounding villages.

Dad began to visit more often, but one night he had to travel on the last train, which was not supposed to stop at Crudgington. The train slowed down, however, while passing through, so Dad jumped out, feeling sure the railway staff would have gone home for the night. Suddenly there was a shout behind him, and a very angry station-master demanded to know what he thought he was doing. He clearly believed Dad hadn't bought a ticket, and in any case jumping from a moving train was - and still is - illegal. Dad noticed the man's strong Welsh accent, so he replied in Welsh, showing his ticket and explaining his plight. There was an instant transformation. He was greeted as *Brawd* - brother - and shaken by the hand. This poor soul had been stranded in England for fifteen years, and the sound of Welsh was as food to the famished. He even offered to lend Dad his bike to cycle to Ellerdine.

On one of his visits, Mrs. Buttery persuaded Dad to go with them to a village dance, his first. He watched, mystified, while the dancers went through the elaborate figures of the Quadrilles and other Old Time dances, but when the band struck up a waltz Mrs. Buttery seized him and he found himself going round and round on the dance floor. When the music stopped she released him, and he fell down. He laughed heartily, but that was the beginning and the end of Dad's dancing career.

During Mum's first year in Ellerdine her mother left Pen-y-Byrwydd and moved to Glochfoel, a small-holding near Berriew - one of the loveliest villages in the County - where she kept hens, geese and a few sheep. Katie continued to live with her.

All this time Dad was looking for somewhere for them to live, preferably a house and shop in Llanidloes. But there was a shortage of houses after World War 1, and for a while he could find nothing. He realised that when properties were for sale they were rarely adertised, because they were snapped up by eager buyers, informed by the local grapevine. So he thought it would help if he could rent a house in Llanidloes where he and Mum could live, and where they would be more likely to have early news of a shop becoming available.

At last, he heard that a house in Smithfield Terrace was vacant. This is a row of cottages at the corner of the Bryndu and Llangurig roads, and the vacant one belonged to one of his relatives near Pantydwr. As soon as he had the news Dad went to visit them. He could hardly wait for the preliminary enquiries about the family to be over before he asked if he could rent the house. But the old man was in no hurry to make up his mind. Dad was pressed to stay for tea, and the table was laid. But he protested that he couldn't eat a crumb. - Nor did he, until the old lady turned on her husband.

"Can't you see he's sick with waiting? Go on! Give him the key!"

So the key was put into his hand, and Dad sat down and made an excellent meal.

During the following months they bought furniture for their home, and the wedding preparations went ahead. They had decided to get married at the beginning of the Summer holidays, but Mum would return to school in September and work her month's notice, this being the only way she could ensure that she received her holiday pay.

The banns were read in Berriew and Llanidloes Parish Churches, but the date of the wedding couldn't be fixed until they knew when Ellerdine school would close, and that depended on when Mr. Adeney, Chairman of the Managers, cut his hay. The first child to arrive at school with the news that 'Mr. Adeney had started cutting' was given a bag of sweets, and the school closed the next day.

Eventually the signal was given and Mum was free to send out the invitations and inform the Rector of Berriew that the wedding would be on August 3rd. It was a small wedding with only the two families invited, and Mum was delighted that the curious only realised a wedding was taking place when they heard the bells at the end, and were just in time to see them coming out.

Before the wedding her mother told her that she and Dad's father had been sweethearts when they were young. It must have seemed strange to both of them when they met again for the first time for many years.

Part of the honeymoon was spent in Wallasey, with Mr. and Mrs. Dumsday and family. Mrs. Dumsday's grandmother had been next-door neighbour to Grandpa and Grandma in Llangurig. The remainder was spent with Mr. and Mrs. Buttery on their farm.

Then they set up home in 2 Smithfield Terrace. Mary sent Dad's piano and he presented it to Mum as a wedding gift. The little house often echoed to its music as their friends gathered round to sing. They were to meet many difficulties, but their love never faltered, and Eric and I grew up in a happy home.

Eventually Dad bought 44 and 45 Long Bridge Street, consisting of 2 shops with living accommodation above each. We moved there when I was 2 years old, and naturally it is the only home that I remember.

Miners at Nant Iago Lead Mine, Pantmawr

Llangurig : Plasynllan (left) and Rock Villas (right)

Wedding of Curigwen Lewis and Andrew Cruickshank

On the right are the bride's brothers, the Rev. Ivor Lewis and Professor E. Arthur Jones, Aberystwyth

By permission of the County Archivist.

Llangurig Council School 1912-14. For details see Appendix

Llanidloes Town Hall 1908

Photo by O'Neill. From Horsfall-Turner's 'Municipal History'

Mrs. Dutton feeding turkeys

The Old Pump, Llanidloes (in use until 1905).
From Horsfall-Turner's 'Municipal History'.

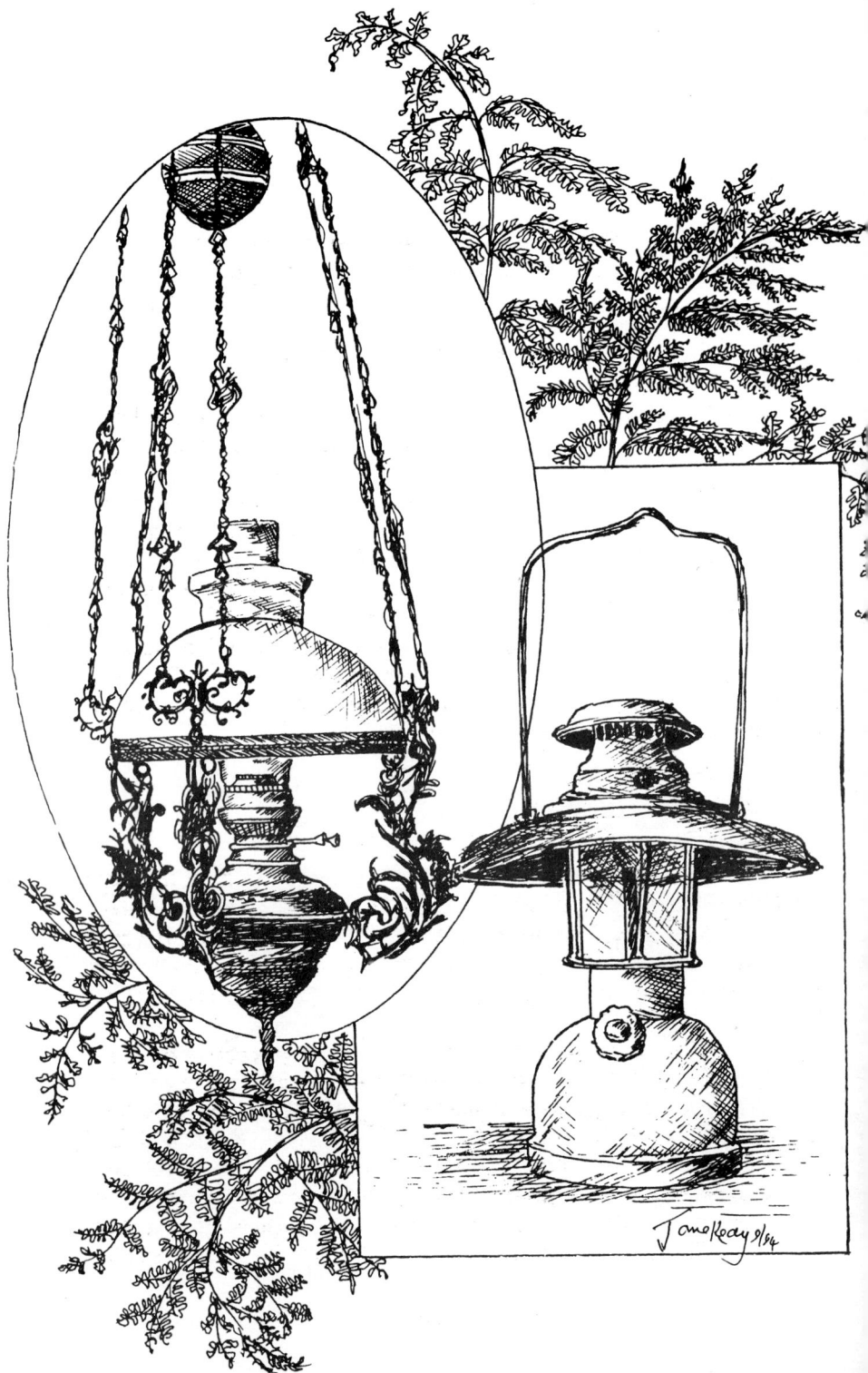

Jane Keay 9/84

Part Three   Annie's Memoirs
[Written by Uncle Johnny's eldest daughter
in 1977]

Introduction

Life in general has changed so much in my life-time that I
have been prompted to write a book and record a few incidents.
The opportunities afforded to children these days and the advance-
ment in home facilities convince me that I had somewhat of a hard
time, quite unknown to myself. Everything I write is true and
dedicated to a devoted mother without whom I could not have faced
up to so many trials. I still follow closely the advice and sound
judgment she gave me, and I am ever grateful.

She was a good mother not in the sense of giving me all I
asked for, but by her example she showed me qualities of fortitude
and courage, and above all a deep sense of faith that God who rules
the Universe should be the head of every home.

Chapter 11   Childhood

My maiden name was Sarah Ann Jones. I was born at Dolau
Cottage in the village of Nantmel, in Radnorshire, on 28th May,
1895. My father, John Jones, was a tailor and my mother, Margaret
Jane, a farmer's daughter, one of a family of 20. They did not all
have the same mother. Ten were step-brothers and sisters and much
older.

When I was three we moved to a larger cottage, quite near,
because my father's business was growing, and he needed to
employ someone. This was one of the results of laying a pipe-line
to carry water from the Elan Valley, some 12 miles away from Dolau
in the Welsh mountains, to Birmingham. Hundreds of workmen
were employed, and they needed accommodation. With only a few
houses around this was a real problem. All our village consisted of
was a Church, a vicarage, a school, a blacksmith's shop, Public

house, about 10 houses with surrounding farms and the Llwyn-barried estate.

My mother usually kept 3 boarders, and we kept a goat to supply us with milk. The drinking water had to be carried half a mile. Water for other purposes was saved in tubs during the winter. In the summer this water also had to be carried. One of the first incidents I can remember was the goat pushing me around. One day she managed to push me into the garden hedge. She gradually became a menace, and it was decided to have her destroyed.

The hide was preserved and was used as a mat in my bedroom. I jumped upon it freely, thinking I was getting my revenge, and that I was master of the situation at last.

My parents were terrified that I would wander away and fall into this deep pipe-line track. An old lady next door kept a strict eye on me, and my mother always told her when she intended going to the clothes-line, or even to the shop. One day I climbed over the gate and this old lady smacked me. I did not approve and I cried bitterly.

To my surprise when I told my mother she supported the old lady, and explained that she was only doing her duty, which was for my benefit. I never forgot it.

There were no children living near and so I had to make my own amusement. I loved the old lady's dog Jumbo. Every bit of food had to be shared with him, and I lay on the mat with my arms around him. No other person attempted to do that.

One day when mother was at the clothes line up some rocks I was left in Dad's armchair. Suddenly a person appeared at the door playing bag-pipes. I screamed and was terrified, having never heard or seen them before. To this day I do not like bag-pipes.

My parents were both musical. Both had very good voices, and were readers of Tonic Solfa. My Dad conducted Mixed and Male-Voice choirs. His one delight was to teach someone to sing. My mother's family composed hymn tunes which often appeared in the Festival books. They discovered when I was about 2 that I had a voice, and a good ear. Naturally Dad started to coach me. It was at this age that he held me up in his arms in Dolau Chapel and I sang **Daddy wouldn't buy me a bow-wow**. From then onwards I continued to sing every time there was a chance, and he was very proud of me.

I was an only child and longed for company. This gave me a liking for animals and birds. In fact, anything that would respond to kindness. All my early life I depended on them for my amusement, and my parents saw to it that I had a pet.

At the age of five I went to school, about half a mile away. On one occasion I ran home, terrified, afraid of a steam roller. For a few mornings my mother had to take me past this monstrous thing.

My Dad had a penny-farthing bicycle. I was allowed to go through the gate to see him mount it from the back. He travelled many miles in this way, and carried suits of clothes to his customers. These suits he made for the small sum of 12 shillings and sixpence, apart from the cost of the material.

At this time, when I was about 6 years old, we moved to a bungalow to give us more accommodation. It was still quite near. It had 4 bedrooms, one large living-room and a room for Dad to store his cloth and cut out his clothes. A sectional workshop was also erected next to the bungalow. By this time his business was booming and he employed 3 workmen. In the new workshop he had 2 sewing machines and a stove to heat the irons. This had previously been done in the house. We also had some land, sufficient to keep a cow, a few sheep and a pig. This was grand as far as I was concerned. The more the merrier. At the age of 7 I was taught to milk the cow, and I also got on good terms with the pig, sufficient to be able to ride on his back occasionally when father was not looking.

Flowers also interested me very much. I made flower beds in ditches. Everything seemed to grow wherever I put it.

I discovered who Father Christmas was, by finding a few sweets, a stocking filled with novelties, a candy pig and a pair of gloves in a basket, tucked away in a remote corner of Dad's cutting room. I said nothing until Christmas morning, when I found the very same things in my stocking, and that lovely myth was no longer.

During the winter evenings the farm servants would gather together in the workshop where they could enjoy warmth and the company of the men. This was a grand opportunity for my Dad to teach them to sing, and I could join them if it was not bed-time. Friday night he would be cutting hair, one after the other. They often gave him an ounce of tobacco.

I discovered one day that I could be of some help to the near-by blacksmith by blowing the bellows and getting the fire going to heat the iron from which the horse shoes were made. The bellows was too high, and he tied a cord to it. I was then able to blow the fire well. We became great friends.

In fact all my friends seemed to be men. Farmers were very kind to me. When they had a weak lamb, perhaps one of 3, I would be given it to feed from a bottle. Once we had 2 lambs, born at night in the snow. In order to warm them up Dad gave one brandy, and mother gave the other peppermint. The latter lived, the former died. Once again mother won. I had great success with bottle feeding by milking the cow straight into a bottle. The milk was then the correct heat for the lamb. When coming home from school it was my reward to see a dear little lamb waiting at the gate, a pussy miaowing or a dog meeting me several yards down the road. Thinking back, people must have felt that I was a lonely little child, always trying to win someone's affection, and have many friends - which I did. This was proved when I was ill. I was showered with gifts of things you would never dream of these days, such as tapioca pudding.

We attended a Baptist chapel. Mother cleaned it, Dad was responsible for the heating and lighting. This was quite a formidable job, trimming and oiling all the lamps. Once a year mother took them home, all the bowls and wicks, boiled them in soda water, and shone them up. While she was dusting the church I had to go into the pulpit, and read a portion of Scripture aloud, recite or sing, in order to become more accustomed to the place, in preparation for the next event.

One afternoon I strolled around the grave-yard, found some ribbons rotting on the graves and picked them up. I took them home, thinking they would do for my dolls if washed and ironed properly. She noticed them and quickly inquired where I had them from. I told her. The result was that I had to take them back and place them on the graves. This entailed a serious lecture about stealing. I was somewhat confused, thinking it was wasteful. She soon convinced me that I was never to interfere with anything that was not my property.

The same thing happened when I found a pheasant's nest in the fields. Finding no daffodils I thought that it would be a fair substitute, and very useful. I also had to take that back.

We attended Chapel 3 times on a Sunday, and my parents did no work on the day, except to feed the animals. All the vegetables were prepared the previous evening. During the week the Sunday-School lesson was prepared and one night each week there was a prayer meeting.

Once a year an Eisteddfod was held to raise funds, and my parents took a big part in this. Dad collected all the prizes, coached competitors and also ran around encouraging competitors to enter. I had to learn the Children's Solo and Recitation. I also tried to get others to compete when I met them in Sunday or day school.

At night I had to read Bible stories before going to bed, and I loved them, especially the stories of Moses, Samuel and Joseph.

I loved going to school, but mother was not satisfied with my knowledge. She would test me sometimes and come to the conclusion that I was wasting my time. On making a few discreet enquiries she discovered that the Head-teachers were usually old, and probably not very interested in getting children on in any way. Quite a number were temporary. Mother was far-sighted and wanted me to have a good education. This worried her although she was doing as much as she could herself, teaching me Needlework, crocheting, singing and playing the harmonium.

The school was Church of England. Scripture was taught by the Vicar, and I brought home a certificate every year. I knew my Bible, but that was all. The vicar discovered that I could sing, and he would collect me from school and take me up to the church to sing for a wedding if a hymn was required because he had to play the organ. This suited me. I loved doing that. I would not join in the Catechism however, on Friday mornings, and I never went to school until it was all over, because my parents, being Baptists, objected. This was quite right, and I am glad they did. I was extremely upset, however, when I discovered that on the day of the Examination the Church scholars were given lemonade and biscuits after we had gone home.

I was now about 10 years old and my Dad built a chicken-house for me. I had 6 hens and a cockerel. I went off to buy food for them, and saw to it that all eggs were paid for, so that I could carry on. This gave me interest and taught me how to use money at an early age.

By this time I could sing quite well. Dad took me on the bar of his ordinary bicycle, having discarded the penny-farthing, to sing at concerts. I also went with him to Eisteddfods where they were taking part. I learned such a lot of good music which came in very useful later. Christmas Day was generally spent in this way, and sometimes we walked miles to and fro. Boxing Day was spent similarly. This was our Christmas, singing all the time. I loved an Eisteddfod, even if I lost, and I mostly did. I found nervousness a severe handicap. I had the voice and the training, but my nerves let me down. My Dad, however, was never discouraged. He knew I would beat the lot some day - and he was right.

On a Saturday, sometimes, he would take me to sing for very old people, or invalids who could not attend concerts. A copper kettle in my possession to this day was given to me on such an occasion. I loved Carol singing too, but I was not allowed to go because the cold air would harm my voice, and I would not then be able to sing in the Chapel.

Memory serves me quite well because I can vaguely remember the Boer War. When an old man delivered newspapers late in the evening everyone was anxiously waiting for news. He slipped on some ice. I laughed, but was quickly reprimanded for this as he might have hurt himself, and he had already walked four miles to bring us the news. In our living room we had pictures of Buller, Baden-Powell and Kitchener who were prominent people in this war. I was led to believe that they were very brave men.

There were also 2 other pictures:- The Broad and Narrow Way, and The Three Parables. These I would study when alone, and I looked up all the references in the Bible. In my mother's bedroom, above her bed, was The Light of The World - Jesus standing outside a locked door. I asked her many questions, the most persistent one being, "Why doesn't He go in?"

My mother's reply was, "It can only be opened from the inside."

When Queen Victoria had her Diamond Jubilee my mother wore a large medal, like a 5 shilling piece, with red, white and blue ribbon.

Another day I shall not forget was the official opening of the Birmingham Water Pipe-line from the Elan Valley, on 21st July 1904. It had taken several years to complete. All school-children attended this occasion. King Edward VII and Queen Alexandra appeared on Rhayader railway platform, and we sang **God Save the King**, and waved our flags merrily. The town was gaily decorated. It was full of men in uniform, bands galore, and plenty of noise.

When King Edward was crowned we all received a mug. Mine, of real china, has his image carved in the base.

My parents were interested in politics and were staunch Liberals. Our representative was Frank Edwards. He usually kept his seat with the exception of one occasion when he lost by 9 votes. Our little village was distressed, but it gave them the urge to work still harder. The Conservative was only in 9 months anyway. It just gave the man time to look round the House of Commons.

Many committees were held in our house, and I had to make myself scarce and go into the workshop or to a neighbour's house. I loved Election time, and boldly wore my Liberal rosette of yellow and purple. I still have a replica of Frank Edwards on a button to wear in my coat. Later on when in my teens I accepted an invitation to join a concert party and gave a concert in his home town. We all stayed in The Cottage which was a large house, and very lovely.

After the concert we had a wonderful spread, and an informal sing-song around the piano. He was a homely man but forth-right. He certainly made an excellent Member of Parliament.

Mother always believed that religion and politics were connected. All these points she carefully explained to me, and she had a grudge against the House of Lords. She felt that they were incompetent men. Their right to sit in the House was handed down to them, irrespective of brains. Every Bill the Commons passed the Lords threw out, or so it seemed.

Disestablishment of the Church was an important measure. I remember my parents, together with many more, refusing to pay the Church rates, and goods of the appropriate value were confiscated. Dad gave up his bicycle, his only means of transport, and others lost their horse and trap.

Lloyd George was a household name of whom all Welsh folk

were proud. He was an eloquent speaker, quick and responsive. I heard him speak, and have shaken hands with him on a platform in Llandrindod Wells.

One day I saw a vehicle go quickly down the road on 4 wheels. It was a motor car, and considered to be very dangerous. It was probably going all of 20 miles an hour. Nevertheless we thought it was wonderful.

Nantmel was stationed 4 miles from Rhayader railway station. Rhayader was our nearest town, and there were no buses or any other kind of public transport. I was now old enough to walk with my mother occasionally, and see some real shops, rather than the village ones - converted front rooms. Sometimes a farmer going to market might pick us up. At other times he might only be able to take one in his trap. This would be a real treat, to have a ride. Mother would buy a joint of meat and several things which we could not obtain in the village.

I always wanted to buy a book in which you could write any amount to settle a debt. This was a cheque book. What I didn't know was that it was geared to a Bank from which money could be drawn, provided that some had been put in. All this had to be explained to me. My parents were never rich enough to have a cheque book, but I had seen other people using one, and thought it was a good idea.

I had been taught to save my money through the Post Office. Gifts of money Mother took charge of on my behalf. It was a happy day when £1 was recorded, and I received a blue paper from the Post Office in my own name.

One day I had gone down to Rhayader in front of my mother, and discovered that the Post Office was being demolished. I thought that my money was lodged there, and I started going home breaking my heart and sobbing as I went until I met her. She quickly comforted me, and once more explained that another building was being erected, and that in the meantime the money was safe in London. I was happy once more.

I placed all my confidence in her. I knew that she was always right. Her word was her bond. If mother promised me anything, good or otherwise I would get it. I have been known to receive punishment two weeks after I had transgressed, so sure was her word. In fact I have placed myself across her knee to get it over. She told me herself.

I have seen her making quilts large enough to cover double sized beds, from cuttings of cloth, sewing them neatly together. In fact she would have a frame in a section of the living room for weeks. I still have such a quilt, and it will last me a life-time. I would never dream of starting on anything like that.

One of the days I can never forget was the Sunday School outing to Aberystwyth, our nearest sea-side town, some 60 miles away. We had to leave Rhayader station at 6.30 a.m. This meant that mother had to be up by 4 a.m. to milk the cow, feed the pig, and get ready to meet our conveyance at the chapel - a brake drawn by two horses. - Oh the excitement and the preparations! We were afraid to over-sleep, and borrowed alarm clocks. We found the finest rose for a button-hole.

It was a joyous day. There were long train rides, paddles, digging in the sands, rides on the donkey. - Marvellous! - Unfortunately it only came every other year. The following year there would be a tea-party and games. If we failed to attend either we received a book. To me a book meant very little. I was not interested.

Music lessons were considered by my parents, but they decided that education in school was far more important. I carried on singing as usual.

Annie's Parents - Margaret Jane and John Jones.

Uncle Johnny's family, friends and workmen.
Back Row : Margaret Jane, Annie (the baby), John Jones and Margaret, Jane's cousin.
Front Row : Johnny's workmen and friends.

Chapter 12   Holidays

By this time I was old enough to go to my Grand-ma on my father's side for my holidays. This was a short train ride from Rhayader to Pant-y-Dwr, another small village. My grandmother was a wonderful person in my estimation. She was present when I was born, and a dear old lady. She wore a lace cap, clean as a new pin. She was kind, and always prepared a little bed for me in her own bedroom. Her bed had 4 posts, and a curtain all around. My grandad's night-cap hung on a frill at the top.

He was a fussy, comical little man, a tailor by trade. His workshop was nothing new to me. I was more interested in going upstairs to bed, and in pumping water into a bucket. At home I always had to bend down and scoop it up with a ladle. The train was an attraction too. I counted the coaches and the trucks. Grandma never allowed me to go down to the station, however, for fear of accidents.

I always spent a few days at my mother's home at Gellidywyll with her brother, Evan. (My other grandma died when I was two, and I do not remember her.) This was an isolated farm house, way up in the hills. There was no other house in sight, and the land was marshy. They had no musical instrument to play. My cousins were much too young for me to play with. My best amusement was to go with my uncle up the mountain, and watch him train a sheep dog. He was a specialist at this, and trained dogs belonging to others, for sheepdog trials. His whistle was most powerful, and it was a revelation to see how these clever animals responded.

Then I would move on to another uncle, Jonathan, at Cenarth Mill. I needed no more than a nod or a wink to go there. It was a most interesting place. I loved to see the mill working, grinding the corn into flour. Uncle was a fine musician, and I had to undergo a few tests in ear and sight reading. It was not surprising that he was an examiner for the Tonic Sol-fa College of Music and its certificates. As he was a relative I did not try for any of the awards.

Unfortunately the mill depended on water. When I was on holiday it was always Summer time. That often meant waiting for the pond to fill up in order for it to drive the wheels.

It grieves me to think that now all these holiday haunts may at some time be flooded, and that I may have seen them for the last time. I hope not.*

My holiday would always end with my grandma. She was one of the best known mid-wives in the district. It was possible for anyone to call her up during the night because of a serious illness, such as pneumonia, or for a confinement. They usually brought a spare pony. She would stay there until the crisis was over. In those days there were no District Nurses, and these mid-wives were most valuable.

Grandad was a tiny, comical man. I liked to play tricks on him, because he was hasty, and talked very quickly. If the cow was in calf it was my job to go for milk to a nearby farm. One evening I played on the road until it was dark, and quite forgot the milk. Seeing a little man coming along with a milk can my mates and I quickly slipped into a field for him to pass. He was talking to himself, going from one ditch to the other, and saying,

"There must be a hedge right across the road," which caused giggles, and he shouted,

"Come on my girl. I know you are there." - His hearing was far better than his sight. - I immediately came to the rescue with my apologies and completed the journey.

If there was a knock at the door and he expected a customer whose clothes were not ready he would say to grandma, "Oh dear! Here we are at the side of the road, and the people are calling all day. You go to them." He would disappear into the back kitchen. Grandma had to face the music and calm the waters.

One of my mother's sisters lived in Llangurig, 9 miles from Rhayader. I was taken by train to Llanidloes, and then I had to walk a further 5 miles. Mother left me for a week, and then spent a few days before we went home together. I had 3 cousins there who were all boys, and just about my own age, (Orlando, Edgar and Victor) and one cousin much older, Margaret Mary, with whom I slept.

Uncle was also a tailor, so there was no interest in that for me, and the boys spoke Welsh to each other. If anyone wanted to

* A reference to the proposal to create a dam in the Dulas Valley. This was defeated.

say something about me it was said in Welsh. This annoyed me, not knowing a word of the language. It was there that I learned to walk on stilts, and thought I was very clever. Needless to say, on my return there was no peace until my Dad had made a pair for me from wood cut out of a hedge. Strangely enough this Uncle Benjamin was an uncle to my Dad. It seems that two sisters, one ten years older than the other, married an uncle and a nephew. It always puzzled me. They were very much alike in looks and ways.

Aunty turned her front room into a shop and sold odds and ends, but like all country shops folks were inclined to gossip. One day Aunty went out for a few minutes and Uncle kept the shop. He knew nothing about it, and got a bit fed up. He said to the next customer, "What do you want, Mrs. Jones?"

She could only reply, "We..ell.."

"You'll have to wait," Uncle said. "Perhaps she has a few minutes to spare for you as well. It's all talk in this place, and nothing seems to get done."

Jane Keay '14

Chapter 13 Village Life

As time went on two problems developed at home. Firstly the rats came up in large numbers from the river bank and settled underneath our bungalow. They were a real nuisance, boring holes, and disturbing our night's rest. We had a very good cat which killed 9 in one day, and laid them on the mat for everyone to see.

Now my mother always salted the bacon every year, and to her amazement she found that the rats had eaten part of one ham. This was serious. Something drastic had to be done. No one liked the idea of laying poison because of all the animals, and so Dad thought he would ask a few farmers who were friends to bring some dogs, a ferret and guns to shoot them. He did not possess a gun himself, but he was a fine shot. He had to borrow a gun, and this he did late one night. Unfortunately the estate keeper caught him carrying the gun without a licence, as well as 3 cartridges in his pocket, which were all his friend had.

Next day the shoot took place and we got rid of all our pests. I'm sure that the poor cat was as relieved as we were.

It did not end there, however, for my father had a summons. This did not worry us unduly, but the way in which he could prove to the magistrates that this shooting was necessary did worry my mother. She solved the problem in her customary way. On the morning of the dreaded day the ham was lifted out of the salt, washed, put in a clean pillow-slip, and taken up to the magistrates' room, and carefully laid on a table.

No sooner had the head magistrate entered than he was heard to say, "Good God! Look at this!"

In a few minutes the case was dismissed, and after a short explanation Dad was free, with no costs to pay.

The other problem was Gypsies. Above the main road we had a small plot of grass surrounded by rocks. A few neighbours had levelled this to play quoits in the summer evenings. Gypsies found this a suitable place to settle their caravans. There was plenty of shade, and a little fresh grass for the horses. They would arrive late on a Saturday evening which meant that we could not all go to

114

church on Sunday. One never knew what they might steal. I had been warned never to bring them into the house, or encourage them in any way.

As usual my mother set to work once again. Her brain was always working. She went into the workshop where there were several young farmers and asked for a volunteer policeman. She knew where there was an old tunic and a helmet, having seen them in a house. These were brought to our home, and before long a new police recruit was ready for action, boots polished, white gloves, a truncheon and even a pocket book and pencil. One rehearsal in the kitchen and he was away, down the fields, so that the approach was made from the main road, and not from our house.

It worked. He sent them out at 10 o'clock at night. Believe me or not, that fellow got a real kick out of it. He entered the Police Force, and my Dad made his wedding suit a few years later.

My father was so kind and generous. He never swore or brought drink into the house. He never went to the local public house, but would drink in Rhayader, when his customers met him to settle their bills. He was loved by everyone. I have seen him leave his job in the workshop and help a farmer hurrying to get his hay in when a thunder storm was approaching. He would travel miles on his bicycle to do a good turn to anyone.

One Friday I came home from school determined to learn the first 12 verses of the 53rd Chapter of Isaiah by Monday morning, because the Headmaster was giving a pair of scissors to the best girl, and a knife to the best boy. It was his favourite portion of Scripture. This I accomplished, but the time was too short to recite it properly, with confidence.

Monday came and we all had a go. Some failed to learn it, and so the old man, who was over 80 years of age said that perhaps it would be better if we had one more week. By that time I went through my paces fit for any competition. The poor old man cried like a child. This disturbed me. I wondered why he cried.

'He was despised and rejected, a Man of Sorrows and acquainted with grief.'

These words were a reality to him, and when spoken by a child brought home more deeply the profound message. My mother was an excellent trainer. I won many prizes in our Eisteddfod, as also did others whom she trained. Where she obtained her knowledge I shall never know, because she only went to school half-time, starting at 8 and finishing at 12 years.

I received my scissors which I treasured for many years.

During that week the Headmaster came to see my mother to tell her how much he enjoyed my reciting, and how impressed he was with me as a child. For 3 months I had helped him greatly with the younger group of children in a separate room. I kept them silent and interested. He strongly advised me to go in for teaching, because I had a gift.

Mother's reactions were far from what he expected. First of all, with great deliberation, she said that she would like me to get some knowledge into my head. - The child knew nothing. - And she wanted me to have a secondary education. To do this I must pass the Scholarship. How could this be done? It so happened that the school-master would be leaving in a few months. That was why he had called. His successor, perhaps, could help.

Off went mother to the vicar and told him the circumstances. He was anxious to do all he could, and gave a favourable account of me. The next thing she did was to obtain a Syllabus from the Education Authority, giving the subjects required. They were Arithmetic, History, Geography, Needlework and Common Things. The vicar promised to coach me in History and Geography if I would go to the vicarage. The new Pupil Teacher just arriving would do the Arithmetic and my mother the Needlework. We all set to work as a team. A map of the British Isles was bought, pasted on to a board, and hung in the kitchen, with all the Counties, County Towns and also the Rivers they stood on, and the industries, if any.

One day before this, my mother had asked me where Liverpool was. I replied,"Somewhere near London."

This put an end to those silly answers. She became furious. I made button-holes until I looked like one, and I dreamt about the Kings of England. It was hard work. If only I could have had Scripture, my favourite subject. 'Common Things' puzzled me. It was a kind of Intelligence test.

I was 13 years old when the Scholarship Day arrived. The vicar sent his horse and trap to take us to Rhayader. It was very kind of him. The combined effort was on its way.

116

The examination was held in the Police Station, of all places, and if there was one person I was afraid of it was a policeman. I knew that the gaol was not far away. All these things played on my mind.

A magistrate's room is hardly the place for nervous children to sit examinations, and I was the only girl. Perhaps I was thinking of my Dad and the rat episode. The chief magistrate was invigilating. He was a dear old soul, with white hair, and did his best to make us feel at home.

I don't think I did very well, really, until I came to the Needlework. Given a small piece of white linen, button, needle and cotton I was happy. My face must have lit up for joy because this was something I really could do, and it was admired by the Invigilator. He said he wished that he had a button-hole like that on his shirt. This made my day, and there is no doubt it won me a Scholarship. I shared top place, and I had 99 marks in Needlework. Needless to say there was jubilation in that little village. I was the 3rd on record to go to the Intermediate School.

Chapter 14   Teenage

I had been promised a bicycle if I passed, as there was no other transport. Full of joy the first place I made for was my Grandma's for a week. 13 years of age, winning a Scholarship - she felt more proud of me than ever. My uncle asked me to sing a solo in Nantgwyn chapel, and I sang **Flee as a bird to your mountain.** My life was really beginning and I was so glad for my dear mother's sake. I was all she had and Goodness knows she had many burdens to bear.

I came home, and the problem of the bicycle arose. We journeyed on foot to Llandrindod Wells, 8 miles away, to see the school, and to make arrangements. The firm known as **Tom Norton's** lent me a fixed-wheel bicycle to learn upon, with the understanding that a new one would be bought.

I learned to ride in a few days, and so did my mother, which was a surprise to everyone. Dad was too nervous to help her. One of the workmen did that. We took the bicycle back, but my mother was very loth to part with it. It would be so useful, and so they offered to sell it at a low price, but Dad could not afford to buy the two.

I decided to fall back on my savings in the Post Office and buy my own. It was a good thing I had been taught to save at an early age. My bicycle was a brand new Raleigh, and I rode it proudly home with my mother following me on her bicycle. We were like two queens. Oh what a day!

As I was leaving home it was time to sell my hens. I gave them back, making a profit of 10 shillings. This came in useful.

When September arrived, off I went. Lodgings had to be found for me during the week with a cousin. She was really a second mother to me. I was given butter, eggs and bacon from home, and 2 shillings and sixpence to buy my own food. This was a real experience for a young girl, and I had to be careful to keep sixpence in case I had a puncture. There was no talk of pocket money or sweets in those days.

Aunty Maggie, as I called her, kept a strict eye on me.

Everything special she had was shared with me. My mother knew I was safe with her all the time. She had 3 small children whom I loved, and all my spare time was spent with them. I joined in the family prayers at night around the fire. Uncle Bert was the first man I ever saw doing housework. He could wash clothes, and cook anything. He was a baker by trade.

I found the school hard, and the homework kept me busy. The new subjects I picked up quite well, but with Arithmetic and others I soon discovered I had missed the foundations, and things I should have learned years before I really didn't know. This hampered my progress and gave me an inferiority complex.

I struggled on, cycling home weekends on a lonely 8 miles of country roads through all weathers, but I grew healthy and strong. Many times I have taken off my shoes and stockings and carried my bike through the stream because the bridge was covered in flood water. I always carried a towel for this purpose. In those days we had oil lamps, the rear one painted red. On a windy night they would go out, leaving you in total darkness. Matches were always a necessity. What a difference today with dynamos!

I loved hockey, and never missed my game, even if I had to put my shoes in a bucket of water afterwards. I had heaps of bruises on my legs, but I could run like a park hare, and generally played Centre or Right Wing.

Before I left the school I became Captain of Hockey, and through a stroke of luck played for Wales once. This game was played in Llandrindod Wells. One of the Welsh team fell ill, and so the school was asked to provide one, and being Captain I was chosen. This was a Red Letter Day for me. I did not play my best, being nervous and excited, and though I ran up to the goal several times my shooting was hopeless, but I did my best.

Every Saturday when at home I would try my hand at cookery, and make whatever the class had prepared during the week. Much of it was encouraging, though I had a very poor stove to work on. In order to make sure that I had all the ingredients I would buy them on the way home. In my Cookery examination I made Irish Stew and Rock Buns. I passed, but with no Distinction I'm afraid.

After the Christmas Term Examinations we had a Strike in our class. The teacher lost our examination papers, and prepared

119

another test, but we refused to do it, as it was not our fault. He fetched the Headmaster. Finally it was decided we should answer one question, and a percentage would be taken from that.

It was in this year that my mother met me out from school on a Friday afternoon to give me the sad news that my Grandma had passed away. I loved her dearly and I would still like to think that my grandchildren love me as much as I loved her, but I don't think this will be so.

I was taken to a shop, and a black coat and hat for the funeral were bought on Monday. I suppose in these days a grandchild would not have attended the funeral. Funerals in Wales have a great importance, and are carried out in a far more emotional manner than in England. The coffin, for example, was always carried by friends, and the bearers were the nearest friends, sometimes relatives, who were all given a black band and tie by the undertaker. It was quite common to see country lanes black with people on their way to the burial ground, and the women carrying the wreaths.

Singing is an important part of the occasion. The Welsh sing them on their way to heaven. If you want to hear some Welsh singing which will send cold shivers down your back, go to a funeral. Everyone loves singing, especially hymns, and this is really a compliment to the departed.

I saw my grandma in her coffin, and placed a bunch of snowdrops on her breast. It did not frighten me, but I was very, very sad, because I adored her. For several days I felt lost, but went back to school and carried on as usual. It did not prevent me from visiting my grandad in the summer, and doing a bit of house-keeping for him.

He and all his brothers lived to a ripe old age, between 80 and 90, some over. My Dad lived to 103, and was the only one of the family to reach 100.

I must not fail to recall the wonderful family who lived in Dolau Farm, opposite the church: Mr. Williams, Senior, incidentally our landlord, his wife, daughter Jessie, son Eddie, and a married daughter, Margaret. To me this was an ideal home and gentleman's farmhouse, beautiful and well furnished.

Jessie Williams was organist and also my Sunday School teacher. Eddie was the Sunday School Superintendent. Mrs.

Williams had the adult women's class, but the old gentleman never went to church. That did not mean that he was not a Christian. He gave the burial ground, and was Trustee and Founder of the Cause. He acted as Caretaker, always on guard, especially when concerts and eisteddfods were held. There were hooligans about in those days, but not vandals. They liked to play little tricks on him, such as carrying his front gate a mile up the lane, and letting someone find it.

They kept three farm servants and a maid, but Miss Williams rolled her sleeves up and was always found working in the morning.

I considered it an honour to go there to tea, when the grandchildren were on holiday - Mary, Jessie Ida and Eddie. Before I went I had my drill in etiquette, namely, "Please," and "Thank you;" not to eat too much, or reach across the table - "Please pass so and so."

To avoid problems I would choose a place near the gingerbread, which was my favourite, and did not forget to thank them for my tea, and I did not talk too much. Children today are not taught manners as we were. The Golden Rule: 'Children should be seen and not heard,' is old-fashioned and a thing of the past.

They would come to my home to tea. On one occasion Jessie wanted to see the bees, but they had retired into the hives, so I suggested she come another time. Jessie however quickly got a stick and stirred them up. The result was disastrous. They all came upon me. I had seven stings in my head, and Mother had three, getting them out. That ended the proceedings for that day, and Miss Williams took them home.

At this farm was a bull, always under control, and a prize one at that. You could put your shirt on the Dolau bull winning a prize in any show. I think the breed was Hereford.

If I happened to go on a Sunday we were allowed in the sitting room, which was like the Holy of Holies, not a cushion out of place. We had to entertain the old folk, singing and playing, then off to church. I was allowed to sit in their pew, right behind the organ.

I always admired a wooden table in the servants' quarters. It was so white from scrubbing, and it puzzled me why I could not get

121

ours like that. I scrubbed it hard, but never succeeded.

It was here that I learned to play croquet, a game I loved very much. I long to play it even now.

Life in the home is so different today. We were always told to go out if visitors arrived, and not to listen to conversations. Now children are allowed to hear everything, and they are in the centre all the time. What annoys me most is the way they dictate to parents, and succeed in getting everything they want, together with everyone's attention.

In 1911, when 16 years old, several important things happened to me.

A Festival of the Empire was held in the Crystal Palace in London. Wales was represented by music. Other countries such as India, Australia, Canada, in fact all the Colonies, displayed their goods. It was fabulous. A choir of several thousands was raised, and one contingent went from Llandrindod. My parents and I were selected to go. We practised for months, and it was then I learned some of the finest works of great men: the Choruses from Handel, Mendelssohn, Elgar, also the Welsh Airs. Every 2 weeks a conductor would come and see how each choir was progressing, and tell us what Mr. Harry Evans, the Guest Conductor, expected from us on the day.

We had to raise funds to pay our fares. This we did by giving concerts in hotels during the summer months. At one of these I sang a solo, and afterwards a lady in the audience came to me and said how much she enjoyed my singing, and advised me to have my voice professionally trained, and go to the College of Music. Many adjudicators had told me this before, but it was impossible - she did not know the circumstances. Afterwards I found out that the lady was no other than Dame Clara Butt. How surprised and thrilled I was!

In September I had the result of the Central Welsh Board Examination, and had passed the Junior, much to my astonishment. It was a case of one thrill upon another.

In the same month we went to London, travelling all night by train to Euston. The proprietor of the Gwalia Hotel had a hotel in London, and he gave us all a full breakfast on arrival. We certainly needed it, and a good wash, as the ladies wore white blouses. Then we walked through the streets. I must say I was terribly disappointed. I thought it was dirty. The buildings were black. As crossing London Bridge we paused to look over, but were soon moved on. Then, partly by Underground, which was dark and horrible, we travelled to Crystal Palace. It was made of glass, a wonderful sight. Over the main arch was written, **Wales The Land of Song.**

We rehearsed all the afternoon and gave a concert in the evening. There were 6,000 voices. I felt proud to be one of them. The orchestra numbered 200, and the audience many thousands. It was really more than I could comprehend. The organ was like thunder, very powerful, with hundreds of stops. The volume of singing and the vibration shook the platform.

I was shaken too. Although I had spent months learning the music, I was too overcome to sing, and for the first time in my life I understood what **King of Kings and Lord of Lords** really meant. Mother said I was pale. She thought I was going to faint. What had happened was my Conversion. During the rendering of the **Hallelujah Chorus** God spoke to me, saying,

"I have given you a voice. Now use it for My Name's Sake."

And there in my heart I made up my mind to do that, for the rest of my life to consecrate myself and the talents which He had given me. It was a memorable day, doubtless the greatest decision I ever made.

When it was all over we journeyed to the station, tired out, but filled with music never to be forgotten. Thank God for those wonderful composers who must have been such dedicated men. We boarded the train at midnight and arrived at Llandrindod Wells at 10 o'clock Sunday morning. I went to my lodgings, and my parents had 8 miles to cycle.

I am sorry this delightful building, the Crystal Palace, was burnt down some years ago. In my imagination I can still see, **Wales The Land of Song.** How delighted I was to be Welsh, and once again represent my country.

When I came home at the weekend I decided to go to the Minister and ask him to baptise me, as I had given my heart to Jesus, and was ready to follow him through the waters of Baptism. This he was delighted to do. This was his first church, and I was his first convert.

The Baptism happened one Sunday afternoon in the River Dulas, a tributary of the Wye. I walked through the fields in my wet clothes, but no one ever suffers any harm through Immersion. I preferred this to the baptistry in the chapel because I wanted to follow Christ's example in the River Jordan.

Church and music have always played a large part in my life, and the hymn I chose was:

'Take my life and let it be
Consecrated, lord, to Thee.
Take my voice and let me sing
Always, only for my King.
Take my moments and my days,
Let them flow in ceaseless praise'

Soon after this I met my first boy friend. He was 4 years older than I was. I rarely met him because I had plenty of studying to do. The idea was dropped.

I tried the Senior Central Welsh Board twice. I failed in 2 subjects the first time, then I dropped one language so that I could concentrate more on Latin. My favourite subjects, Scripture and Botany were not on the curriculum. When the examination time came I was terribly unlucky. It was very hot weather and I was not well. I fainted one afternoon, after only answering one question. Because of this I had to pass in 6 subjects, and I only passed in 5, but I surprised myself by getting a very good mark in Mathematics.

The examination worried me so much that my hair turned grey in a few weeks. I just couldn't bear this, and so I bought some dye in a chemist's and tried to do something about it. I never dreamt anyone would notice it, but of course my mother detected it in a few minutes, and I had one of the biggest lectures of my life. I belonged to a family who went grey young, including herself, and this was no disgrace. What I had to do was to see that my character was white too. I never attempted to try that lark again.

My mind was taken off everything by knowing that we were shortly going to move 2 miles nearer Rhayader, to a much nicer house. I helped through my summer holidays and enjoyed every minute of it, trying my hand at painting and decorating.

Then the 1914 War broke out on August 4th. Many of my relatives and friends were called up in the Territorials, and went out to the Dardanelles. One of my cousins was with us on holiday, and he introduced whist to us by bringing a pack of cards. Up to this time I had not been allowed to play. Mother did not like to ban the game entirely, and we were enjoying ourselves when another cousin, working in the trade, was called up late at night, and he had to be ready to join his Regiment at 5 o'clock in the morning. We stayed up all night, putting together all his requirements. Poor boy! He was worried and never appeared likely to ever make a soldier, and had joined the Territorials because of the camp each summer.

We were quickly rationed with food, and the bread was really bad. Undoubtedly this War had brought a gloom upon every-one, and I for once felt glad to be a girl. My cousin (Margaret Mary) invited me to Hengoed in South Wales, and I had a marvel-lous holiday which lasted 6 weeks. I went to Cardiff, Bargoed, Ebw Vale and several other towns. I saw a Woolworths for the first time. If my pocket would have allowed me I would have been loaded with goods.

When I came home Mother fell ill, and I had to do all the work, which was far more than I had realised, such as washing, and butter-making. We were 5 in family - 2 workmen - but we did not have to carry the water so far. All hot water had to be heated on the fire and we had no cooking facilities except an oil stove. The fire ovens were useless. It was once a public house but the licence had been taken away. It was built of stone with a supply of water at the back door. Unfortunately this ran under the house, and it kept the larder very damp.

I enjoyed going upstairs to bed. There were 4 bedrooms, a kitchen, parlour, and a very large scullery. The toilet was still out in the field, but that was not unusual in the country. Apart from that it was a nice house especially in summer time, and it had a good garden. There were several fruit trees, far more land and out-buildings. There was even a stable, but no horse. We kept coal in one part, and any visitor could stable a horse if required.

Sometimes we had 20 sheep, two cows, and always a pig. Everyone who came just loved the situation. It was called Gaufron Villa. I could still enjoy village life. In one of our fields was an Anglican Church, and a few yards further a school, and also a small shop.

Chapter 15   My Teaching Career

In January 1915 I commenced teaching in Howey School. An application form was sent to me by my cousin Henry, who knew two of the school managers very well. I consulted my Headmaster in Llandrindod. He gave me a good reference, and said I had passed in every subject required. How delighted I was at obtaining a post so quickly and near home. It was a little village 1 mile out of Llandrindod Wells, on the Builth road, and I knew many of the people from my school days. In fact several were in the choir which went to London, and my cousin was Choirmaster in the Baptist Church.

I was well advised not to stay in the village, and so I cycled one mile, morning and evening, managing with sandwiches at lunchtime. Everyone was very friendly, and the Headmaster most helpful. It was a very old school, with 46 children on roll. I shared a room with him, and the younger children were in a small room separated by a partition. Having had no teaching practice, the first week I just looked on while the Head demonstrated what he would like me to do.

I fitted into my position like a piece into a jigsaw puzzle. He could not sing, but was very fond of music, and so I took all the music. There was no instrument in the school, and I had to manage with my voice and a pitch fork (or tuning fork) which would give me any key. I also taught all the Needlework while he took the boys in Drawing on Monday and Friday afternoons. There seemed to be very little material. I asked him for more, which he supplied, and we commenced to cut out a few garments. Things progressed favourably. I was extremely happy there. The Headmaster was a fine man. He was prepared to punish for misbehaviour when a child was sent to him.

The War was in full swing, soldiers everywhere, marching along the roads.

The only difficulty I had was the Catechism. This was a Church school, and being a Baptist I could not conscientiously teach

126

a child what I did not believe. The Headmaster said that I need not worry about that.

"Every Friday your class can join mine after the Scripture lesson."

Every morning I taught Scripture, and prepared them for the Scripture examination once a year.

One morning the vicar came in and said I must leave because I was not C. of E., and he called a managers' meeting to carry out his wish. Quite unknown to me the Headmaster intervened, and wrote a letter on my behalf, pleading for me to continue. The vicar lost the day.

As time advanced I discovered these children had wonderful voices. I suggested we gave a concert occasionally to buy some wool for the girls to knit for the soldiers as a War effort. The Head being a sensible man, this was granted, and I set to work finding action songs, solos and recitations. I even went in to the younger children every Wednesday morning to teach them.

In the village there was a working party run by the Mothers' Union with the vicar's wife in charge. It seems this became a gossip group, and it all broke up. Soon afterwards the vicar's wife came to see me concerning the girls' knitting up the wool and carrying on. Every Friday afternoon I took a bundle to the vicarage, and the children and parents were delighted, as we all seemed to have a hand in winning the War.

The concerts were a success. The little Church room was packed and the charge sixpence. I even went further, and took them into competition, and they won several first prizes. These were truly happy days, and the Headmaster told me that if I wanted to compete in an Eisteddfod I could have the day off, as it boosted the children's morale, besides sometimes I brought back the prize to school, and I always had to sing the test piece for them. What I would have done if I had lost I dread to think, but it never happened. During this year I competed in the Welsh National Eisteddfod. My Dad was certain I could not win, but wanted me to have the experience. He came with me to Neath.

My favourite cousin, Herbert, was killed on October 9th, 1917. He was an expert letter-writer. He was the young man who was with us playing cards when the World War broke out. He gave his

127

last cigarette to Stewart, the Territorial who was called up. Stewart went right through the War, but Herbert was killed by a sniper before he reached the front line. I was terribly upset. He was like a brother to me.

In 1918 World War 1 ended, on the eleventh hour of the eleventh day of the eleventh month. There were great rejoicings everywhere. School closed at mid-day. Llandrindod was alive with people, bands, bonfires on the hills, the public houses full to over-flowing. Church services continued until the early hours next day. We were all exhausted.

In 1918 I met a certain young man during a concert, who was to be my future husband. He was on leave from Germany, and returned the next week. I knew all his family who lived in Rhayader, and his brother was my cousin's boy friend. His name was Robert Ernest Davies, and he seemed to have all the qualifications I was looking for. He was smart, fond of music, and he did not drink. This friendship quickly developed. Being apart hastened our engagement in 1919 and on October 12th 1920 we were married.

In one way I felt sad, having to leave the children and all my friends. The vicar and his wife came to the school to congratulate me. They wondered if I could stay on afterwards, like the Primary teacher, but I told them this was impossible. My husband would be returning to a business in South Wales after being demobilised. I understand, however, that they were the first to start a testimonial. In September 1920 I left, but returned a little later to receive a clock, given by the staff, managers, scholars and friends, and that clock is still ticking in my sitting room. The Primary class also gave me a silver pin tray .I found it very difficult to say even a few words, being quite overcome. The Headmaster requested that I should sing his favourite solo, **Friends** by Clara Novello Davies.

My parents, though delighted about my marriage, arranged to adopt a little girl of 9, who was in need of a foster mother, and she proved to be a great help in many ways.

It was a lovely wedding. At 8.30 a.m. on 1st October 1920, in Rhayader Baptist Church, very early, but not too early for a crowd of well-wishers to attend. I wore a mauve crepe-de-chine dress, and a hand-made hat to match. This was my favourite colour. Having white hair and little colour, white would make me look worse.

I chose to have 2 young brides-maids, dressed in white with little veils.

There were about 40 guests. Two wedding cakes were given me by a baker in Howey, and one was placed on his counter in the shop so that the children could participate. The honeymoon was spent in Blackpool and Manchester. We had to return rather quickly because a choir in Llandrindod were giving me a presentation. This was a biscuit barrel, suitably inscribed, all over the silver lid.

Annie - My father's cousin.

Annie's Wedding to Robert Davies.

Chapter 16   Family Changes

Our new home was in Cwm Felinfach, Monmouthshire, a mining town. It was there that I had my first experience of living among miners. I did not even know my friends when their faces were black. They all looked so alike.

One morning I heard a strange hooter, and discovered it was a pit disaster. All the women were running with babies in their arms, terrified. No one knew who was missing until the cage came up. Even though it was a 'small' disaster it gave me an idea of what these brave men face up to every day.

Unfortunately for me my mother's health broke up. She had a terrible fall, so we decided to go back to Rhayader, to open a business at my husband's home and live at my home. My stay in Cwm Felinfach was very short.

In 1921 my first child was born, William John Cenarth, a bouncing boy of 9 pounds. My Dad was very excited. He wanted a boy, hence the name John was given. Cenarth was the name of the hill by my mother's home, William my husband's father's name. He was a happy, contented child. I scarcely knew I had a baby. He could be left with anyone. But it took me a long time to recover and regain my usual strength.

One day my grandad, now 90 years of age, came by train from Pantydwr to Rhayader to have his photograph taken with us, making 4 generations. In order to comply with the photographer's time we had to wake Cenarth up from his sleep, and he strongly disapproved. Only by putting brown sugar on a dummy could we stop him crying. It was a shame because he was such a happy baby.

The trials of married life were just beginning for me. Very soon we heard that the house was to be sold. There was a great upheaval. We were all sorry, at the same time realising how with my mother's illness it could be for the best.

When Cenarth was 1½ years old my mother died, and was laid to rest in Nantgwyn graveyard, near her home. She died on 10th February, 1923, only 55 years old. She loved her grandchild dearly. He could recite 2 verses of **Gentle Jesus, meek and mild** for her and did so every evening as he went to bed.

Dark clouds hovered over us for several months. We missed her more than words can express. In fact I was so busy concentrating on my tasks that I did not fully realise my loss for a long time. Cenarth helped us all. He was so amusing and very quick learning Nursery Rhymes, in fact, anything. In the tailor's shop Dad taught him to sit on the table like them, and even gave him a piece of material to sew.

He went to Sunday School very early and at the age of 2 he had a prize for good attendance, and recited in the Christmas entertainment, **A Child's Prayer**, which should have been,**Gentle Jesus**. When put on the platform, however, Cenarth said,

'Pussy cat, Pussy cat, where have you been?'

This raised a huge laugh from the congregation. Poor little chap. He got mixed up, and no wonder with so many people teaching him so many different things.

My Dad worshipped him, and made his idol a beautiful naval overcoat of the best navy serge. It was the talk of the town. Orders poured in from all parts of the town, but he would not make another. It was only for his grandchild.

Life was becoming more and more difficult with 2 families to look after, and 2 businesses. I was thankful for May, the adopted girl who was growing up to be extremely useful.

We went jogging along in this way for about 2 years, until my father married again. Then I felt more free.

We lost no time in finding a suitable house with a shop in Rhayader, on the banks of the River Wye. It was an unwieldy place, 3 storeys high, with a large cellar and far too many stairs. There was only one very small living room on the floor behind the shop. At least it was a home, and the 3 of us were together on our own for the first time.

My Dad now had a family to support. Children kept arriving, though he was over 60 when he remarried. It was almost unbelievable. His wife was my own age, very different from my mother, but very kind to him, and they brought up 6 healthy children, all younger than Cenarth. To me this was astounding.

On October 4th 1926 my second child, Howell George, was

born, not so bonny as Cen, but perfectly healthy. I was grateful when that was over, because we had lost my mother, and I wondered what I should do. I need not have done so, because my mother-in-law stepped in, having had 7 of her own. I never wanted for anything.

Business was not improving. Rather than lose any more money we decided to give it up, and live on my husband's part time job as a Relieving Officer, supplemented by boarders.

During the winter of 1929 we had a long spell of frost and snow. The River Wye was frozen over for 13 weeks. Cenarth and five of his school mates had a very narrow escape, having crossed over the river at the deepest point just before the ice gave way, and we parents were extremely thankful. The children did not tell us. It was the folk who lived on the bank, and heard the crash.

Water was always an attraction to Cen. He managed to get his feet wet continually. He also liked climbing trees. This kept me busy mending the seat of his trousers, and he never knew what the word 'danger' meant. (Cenarth had a successful Naval career.)

In 1930 my husband applied for a better post in Oswestry, Shropshire. He was successful. The salary was more, as there was quite a large district to cover, and so a new phase of our lives began.

The Four Generations :

Annie with baby Cenarth, her father and grandfather, William Jones.

Epilogue

A Ripe Old Age

Grandpa lived to be 91, the longest-lived of all the brothers, and on his 90th Birthday he chuckled as he remarked, "Little Benjamin has beaten them all."

Uncle Johnny - Annie's father - was even more remarkable, living to be 103. He was 73 years old when his youngest child was born, and he lived to see eleven grand-children and 2 great- grand-children.

At the age of 80, during World War 11, he joined the Doldowlod unit of the Home Guard - becoming the oldest Home Guard in the country.

"I used to go on maneouvres with them," he recalled, "and beat them hollow at marching from Doldowlod to Llanidloes, and I never used spectacles when firing." In fact he could read a news-paper without spectacles when he was 100.

Singing with the Rhayader Male Voice Choir, he became a soloist at the National Eisteddfod, and at the age of 91 he sang, "Bless this House," as a solo with the choir backing, on a record made by the BBC.

In 1953 when Queen Elizabeth came to open the Claerwen Dam he conducted the Rhayader Choir and sang for her. He was then 93 years old.

At 95 he underwent 2 major operations, and nearly caused a fire in the hospital by smoking his pipe under the sheets.

He retained all his faculties to the end. - He could read without glasses, hear without any aid, and had no dentures. The latter he was determined not to have because, "God never intended us to have such things."

When he was 100 he was asked the secret of his long life. He said, "Try it. - Plenty to eat, plenty to drink, a little smoke, two good wives, and most of all a contented mind. - Never worry about anything."

Later History of Pantmawr

In 1921, the Verney family sold the Clochfaen estate and left the district. Colonel and Mrs. Verney had lavished money on the rebuilding of most of the village, providing a good water supply, converting the Black Lion from a public house into an attractive hotel, and advertising Llangurig as a desirable tourist centre, with boating on the lake just outside the village, shooting and fishing. But times were hard in the post-war years, and few visitors came. Moreover agricultural prices were disastrously low. Their son Harry and his wife, Lady Joan, found it impossible to continue keeping their estate in Wales as well as those in England.

Naturally the agricultural depression affected the smaller farmers even more harshly. Unemployment rose as farmers found themselves unable to afford labourers. Rural depopulation began to cast a blight on the area.

By 1926 Pantmawr school had dwindled to 5 pupils, and the authorities decided to close the school, and transport the pupils to Llangurig. Mr. Bill Jones of Rhosgoch was one of the five - he was then 8 years old. He remembers Uncle Edgar as the first taxi employed to take them, and he believes that Pantmawr may have been the first school in Wales to close, and Uncle's car to have been the first School Transport.

He recalls:

"In those times we had a Vicar, a preacher, a policeman, a tailor, a blacksmith, a wheelwright, two shops and two pubs. They've pretty well all gone except the one shop and the two pubs. The school has picked up a little since some more houses have been built, but it's been in danger of closing.

"They were good days. Though they were poor, people were friendly. They used to visit each other's houses regularly, which isn't done much now. And they used to go to chapel. My grandfather used to go to Capel Uchaf. The church, too, was full in those days - up to the early 1940s.

"Llangurig Eisteddfod was still going when I was young. William Price used to conduct the Choir. He was a strict conductor. He used to conduct the singing in the Methodist Chapel, where it was held. It was a big Eisteddfod for the size of the village, but they held Eisteddfods in Dernol and Cwmbelan, and it was packed - as many outside as inside.

"When I was in school there were only two families in the village who didn't speak Welsh, and when I was old enough to go to a pub, the conversation was all in Welsh.

"People used to walk to Chapel miles and miles. I remember old Richard Davies Ty Cwm used to walk down, on Sunday evening mostly, on his way to the Wesleyans. - He was a big Wesleyan, and he used to take part in the services. He used to practise on the way down, and we could hear him practising praying to himself. I can see him now. He used to start early, then he would stop and turn around and you could hear him preaching to himself there. He was very earnest.

"The Lewises were in Nanty Farm, opposite the Glansevern Arms. I can just remember old Mr. Lewis, Professor Lewis' father. He died and then after Mrs. Lewis died it was sold to the Forestry Commission. That was the first farm the Commission bought, and the first trees were planted in 1929 - the first trees in the area if not in Wales. - Then over the years other areas like Hafren Forest were planted, mostly in the 1930s. They were poor times, and people were glad to sell the land, or at least they found they had to." He laments the afforestation - the monotony -

"It's the same old thing for miles and miles and miles. You can go from here now and down to Rhandirmwyn, Llandovery way, and not come out of the Forestry. Except for the odd little piece it's Forestry all the way." - the loss of the community -

"The only little places they have sold have been sold to incomers, for holiday homes mostly, though some are living there." - and the loss of the wild life. -

"What do you see in the forest? Nothing but foxes. Owls? I haven't seen one for about 2 years. Haven't heard one, which is more to the point, for you used to hear them when you couldn't see them. There are very few owls about, I'm afraid. They've got nothing to feed on. They've lost the ground, the rushes and the long grasses where they were hunting mice. People say to me, 'There are no buzzards.' Well, there are no sheep on these hills. When you've got thousands of sheep there are bound to be carcasses, and the buzzards fed on those. In the lowlands of course you've got to bury them, but when they were on the hills you didn't know where they were."

I asked him if there were still otters in the river, and he sadly shook his head.

"There are no fish there now. It's absolutely dead."I could hardly believe it. This is the River Wye, not far from its source, above Llangurig, the first vilage on the Wye.

"There's very few fish from here to Rhayader. I've got a son in Rhayader and he's not had a fish for ages, and he used to go fishing. It was famous for salmon and trout. I used to catch beautiful trout in the River Wye or the Bidno or the little streams. There was never any shortage. But there's no growth on the rivers - no weeds, because there's no oxygen there. - That's what kills the fish and the growth. You would see the weeds by the side of the river, and the feed for the fish was in there, the flies and other insects."

In his opinion the cause is acid rain - again the fault of the forestry.

Even more ominous is the sale of large portions of the forest to private interests. These are run by forestry firms in which individuals invest in order to avoid tax. He describes how they are sometimes brought over by helicopter to see the section which belongs to them. Such divided ownership makes it very difficult to find out to whom a particular part belongs. So it is now harder than ever to protect rights-of-way.

Not even the Local Authorities can be relied on to do so. The road past the beauty spot to which he had referred used to cross a bridge from Montgomeryshire into Radnorshire, the two Counties sharing the cost of its upkeep. Now the bridge has fallen, and no one is concerned to re-erect it and so maintain the old Drovers' road along which the miners used to walk to Pantmawr.

As he sums up his experience -

"Things have changed dramatically in my time."

Mr. Jones is a member of a family who have lived on the same farm for generations, at least two centuries. There are not many such families left in the area.

But he is not idealising the past. Though he shudders at the thought of 20 to 30 windmills on his favourite beauty spot from which on a clear day you can see the Elan Valley and right down to the Brecon Beacons, he admits that it might be better than using nuclear energy. Nor would he wish to bring back lead mining, with its toll of early deaths from poisoning.

But the loss he laments is real - the destruction of the environment, and the gradual disappearance of a living community.

Old friends meet again : Grandfather with Mrs. Williams.

The Oldest Home Guard in Britain : Uncle Johnny, aged 80.

John Jones, aged 92 years, singing at the opening of the Claerwen Reservoir by Queen Elizabeth II in 1953. Gerald Morgan conducting.

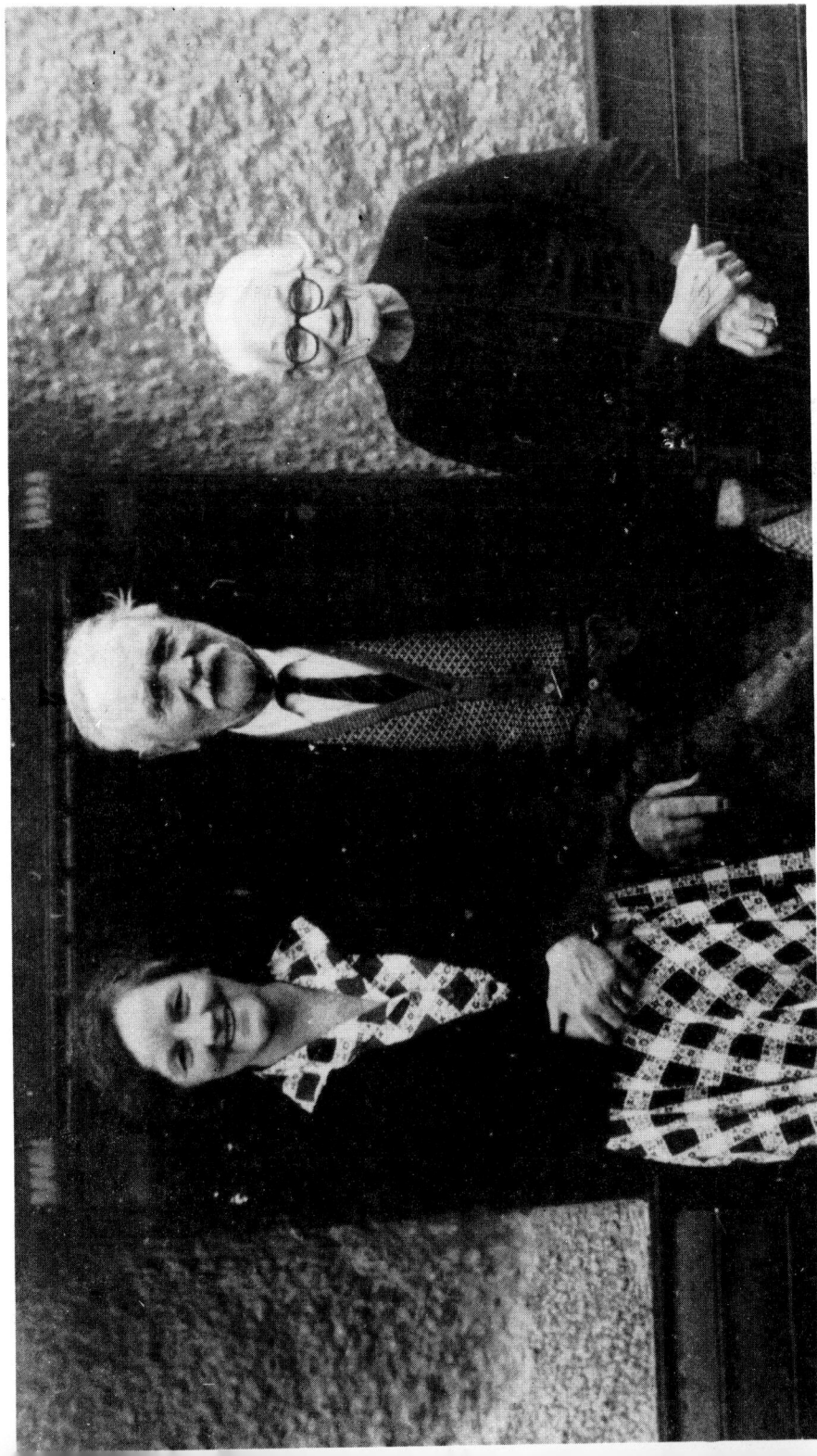

Uncle Johnny, aged 100 with Mrs. Harries and her mother, Mrs. Tomlins.

Notes

1.   Examples of Sums
If a pair of shoes cost 4s 6d what is the value of 12 dozen?
If a gentleman's income is £500 a year and he spends
19/4 per day, how much does he lay by at the year's end?
If I buy 14 yards of cloth for 10 guineas, how many Flemish ells
can I buy for £288/17/6?
If one English ell, 2 quarters, cost 4/7 what will 39½ cost at the
same rate?
A gentleman bought a wedge of gold which weighed 14 lb 3 oz 8
dwts, for the sum of £514/14s. At what rate did he pay for it per
ounce?
A grocer bought 4 hogs heads of sugar each weighing neat 6 cwt 2
qrs 14 lb, which cost him £2/8/6 per cwt. What is the value of 4
hogs heads?
A gentleman hath an annuity of £876/17 per annum. I desire to
know how much he may spend daily, that at the year's end he may
lay up 200 guineas, and give to the poor quarterly 40 Moidores.
2.   The Humphreys Owen family held an estate in the Llangurig
area, and also at Glan-Severn near Berriew.
This accounts for the existence of the Glan-Severn Arms Hotel
beyond Pantmawr, on the banks of the Wye. Arthur Charles
Humphreys Owen became the first Chairman of Montgomeryshire
County Council. It was largely through his efforts that Wales obtained a system of Secondary education, the County Intermediate
Schools. He was also a benefactor of the University of Wales, and
endowed scholarships for students.
3.   See **Report of the Charity Commissioners, 1899**
4.   **Montgomeryshire Collections Vol.3,1870**
5.   Ibid
6.   For the development of the New Clochfaen and the Restoration of the Parish Church see illustrated articles by James Stirk
and Roy Fenn (**Montgomeryshire Collections Vol.75, 1987**) and
James Stirk (**Ibid, Vol. 77,1989**)
    The lithograph of the Parish Church is based on E.Salter's paint-
ing. See **Mont.Col. vol.79,1991** for reproduction of painting and
notes.
7.   See **Report of the Charity Commissioners, 1899**

8. See **Rebirth of a Nation: Wales 1880 - 1980**
by Prof. Kenneth Morgan. (OUP) pp.146-148.
also **Wales! Wales!** by Dr. Dai Smith:
Essay: **A Place in South Wales** (Allen & Unwin)
9. See **Kerry - The Church and the Village**
by Mr. Noel Jerman, C.B.E., M.A.,F.S.A.
10. This was John Wilkes Poundley, grandson of J.W.Poundley, Architect and Surveyor, who was instrumental in the creation of the Abermule and Kerry Railway. The grandson, Jack, a skilful amateur photographer, left a fine series of photographs of old Kerry characters, taken 1915 - 1920. (Originals in the National Library, Aberystwyth. Copies in Newtown Textile Museum.) Also an album, 'Sunny Memories' 1914 - 18, in the National Library. Unfortunately no copy of the Maypole and Morris Dancers has been located.
11. Squire Willans' generosity to the school was entirely in keeping with his life and character:
'He was a country gentleman of cultured tastes, high ideals, deep faith and astounding generosity.
'He was a County Councillor for over 50 years, High Sheriff of Montgomeryshire in 1927, a J.P., Member of the Governing bodies of the University Colleges at Aberystwyth, Bangor and Cardiff, and of the National Library of Wales and the National Museum.
'His greatest pleasure came from encouraging and helping young boys of the village, and young students from Aberystwyth College, especially those recommended by his great friend Professor Fleur, to share his interests. Among those who owe much to him are such distinguished scholars as Emeritus Professors E.G.Bowen, Estyn Evans, Arthur Davies, Dr. Iorwerth Peate and Dr. Colin Easthope'
[From **Archaeologia Cambrensis, 1982** - Presidential Address by Mr. Noel Jerman, C.B.E., M.A., F.S.A.]
12. Mr. Noel Jerman took his B.A. in Geography at Aberystwyth. His M.A. thesis was on the Archaeology of East Central Wales. He took part in several important excavations. In 1946 he obtained a permanent post in the Civil Service in London. In 1951 he was moved to Cardiff and began there his long and distinguished service to the Welsh Office.
Dr. Colin Easthope became Senior Lecturer in Mathematics at

University College of Wales, Aberystwyth.

13. See Manuscript **Notes towards a History of Llandinam** in the Cecil Bennet Vaughan Collection, National Library of Wales.

14. Rhai Atgofion Yr Hen Ysgol, Pantmawr, Llangurig by Professor E.Arthur Lewis. Translated by Mr. E. Ronald Morris, B.A

Dr. Lewis became the first Professor of Welsh History at the University College of Wales, Aberystwyth. His pioneering research laid the foundations of this subject.

His brother, Rev. Ifor Lewis, was also a brilliant scholar. Their half-sister, Curigwen Lewis, was a talented actress, and married Andrew Cruikshank . I am indebted to Mrs. Cruikshank for permission to quote from Dr. Lewis' book.

15. Harry Lloyd Verney, son of Colonel and Mrs. Lloyd Verney, married Lady Joan Cuffe, eldest daughter of the Earl of Desart. He was Deputy Master of the Household of Edward V11, and afterwards Groom-in-Waiting to George V. He acted as Private Secretary to Queen Mary, to whom Lady Joan was Lady-in-Waiting.

In 1917 Prince Albert (later King George V1) spent some time at Clochfaen recuperating from a spell of illness. The place where he sat in the Parish Church is marked.

Although the Verneys have long left the district, in 1983 when the Church needed a new roof, the Queen Mother sent a tea service which was raffled, raising a handsome amount of money.

Bibliography

1. **The Montgomeryshire Collections**, published by the Powysland Club, volumes 3, 75, 77 and 79.
2. **Report of the Charity Commissioners, 1899**
3. **Rebirth of a Nation: Wales 1880 - 1980** by Professor Kenneth O. Morgan. (O.U.P.)
4. **Wales! Wales!** by Dr. Dai Smith (Allen & Unwin)
5. **Education in a Welsh Rural County 1870 - 1973** by Dr. J.A.Davies (University of Wales Press)
6. The Cecil Vaughan Owen Manuscript Collection at the National Library of Wales, Aberystwyth.
7. **Kerry: The Church and the Village** by Noel Jerman, C.B.E., M.A., F.S.A.
8. **Rhai Atgofion Yr Hen Ysgol, Pantmawr, Llangurig** by Dr.E Arthur Lewis. (trans. by E.Ronald Morris, B.A.)
9. **Archaeologia Cambrensis**: Journal of the Cambrian Archaeological Association. (1982)
10. **The Photographer in Rural Wales** by Dr.W.T.R.Pryce. (Powysland Club, 1991)
11. **John Thomas, 1838 - 1905, Photographer** by H.Woollen and A.Crawford. (Gomer Press)
12 Log Books and Registers of Castle Caereinion, Kerry and Llandinam Primary Schools, by kind permission of the Governors and Headmasters.
13. Log Books and Registers of Llangurig, Dolforwyn and Pantmawr Primary Schools at the Powys County Archives, by kind permission of the County Archivist.
14. Newspapers of the period at the Newtown Branch of the Powys County Library and the Libraries at Bargoed and Merthyr Tydfil.

END

APPENDIX

Shearing at Ystradolwyn Farm, Cwmbelan.

Front row, left to right: Elwyn Jones; Tommy, Ystradolwyn; Lewis Davies, Cwmdulas; Tom Davies, Gellifawr; George Davies, Hafodffraith; Edward Evans, Ystradolwyn; John Evans, Wern Cottage; Bill Evans, Penwern.

Second row, left to right:- Edward George Hafodffraith; John Brown, Bwlch hafod y gog; Leonard Jones, Tyllewelyn; Richie Evans, Ystradolwyn; -

Llangurig Council School (Girls) about 1912-14

Front row, left to right: Gwladys Griffiths, Cilgwrgan Fach; Elizabeth Jane Jones, Bidno Mill; Dilys Church, Wesley Row; - Davies, Pantgwyn; Mary Thomas, Tynddol; Peggy Turner, Maesmawr; Anne Turner, Maesmawr.

Second row, left to right: Ada Turner, Bryncylla; - Davies, Pantgwyn; Lizzie Ann Turner, Bryncylla; Esther Morgan, Chapel House; -; Lucy Hughes, Penycroesau; Phyllis Price, Bronwig; Betty Evans, Maesydwri; Lena Turner, Maesmawr; Annie Jones, Waun.

Third row, left to right : Eunice Davies, Tynymaes; Cissie Welson, Hafodlydau; Anne (Nancy) Davies, Clochfaen Farm; Maggie Mills, Green Terrace; Edith Pryce, Brongurig; Beatrice Rowlands, Nantgwyllt; Priscilla Thomas, Tynddol; Dorothy Lowell, Clochfaen Cottages; Miss Patti Jones (Assistant) later Mrs. Jane Griffiths, Pengeulan.

Back row, left to right: Mr Rowbotham (Headmaster); Mr. Hugh Peter Jones (Assistant); Elsie Jones, Ochr Deildre; Gwen Pryce, Cilgwrgan; Muriel Welson, Hafodlydau (later Mrs. J.Ellis, Printer); Ann Griffiths, Cilgwrgan Fach; Gladys Jones, Bidno Mill; Gladys Thomas, Tynddol; Jane Rees, (later Mrs. W.Davies); Evelyn Davies, Top Shop.